SELECTED POEMS OF HERMAN MELVILLE

Selected Poems of
HERMAN MELVILLE

Edited by HENNIG COHEN

FORDHAM UNIVERSITY PRESS
New York

Second Printing 1992

Library of Congress Cataloging-in-Publication Data

Melville, Herman.
  [Poems. Selections]
  Selected poems of Herman Melville / Edited by Hennig Cohen.
     p.   cm.
  ISBN 0-8232-1336-6 (pbk.)
  I. Cohen, Hennig. II. Title.
PS2382.C6   1991
811'.3—dc20   91-55378
                                               CIP

The material from Herman Melville's JOURNAL OF
A VISIT TO EUROPE AND THE LEVANT, edited by
Howard C. Horsford, Copyright 1955 Princeton
University Press, is quoted by permission from
Princeton University Press.

Acknowledgments

The text of *Selected Poems of Herman Melville* is based upon first editions of *Battle-Pieces and Aspects of the War* (1866), *Clarel: A Poem and Pilgrimage in the Holy Land* (1876), *John Marr and Other Sailors with Some Sea-Pieces* (1888), *Timoleon Etc.* (1891) and, for the poetry unpublished at the time of his death, upon Melville's manuscripts. To establish the text I made use of copies of *John Marr* and *Timoleon* in the University of Texas Library, of *Clarel* in the Library Company of Philadelphia, and of the Melville manuscript collection in the Houghton Library of Harvard University. For permission to use these materials I am very grateful. I also wish to acknowledge the kindness of the Princeton University Press for permission to quote from Melville's *Journal of a Visit to Europe and the Levant: October 11, 1856–May 6, 1857* (1955), edited by Howard C. Horsford.

Among the many students of Melville whose contributions are reflected in this book, I should like to state my particular indebtedness to Howard Vincent, Merton M. Sealts, Richard H. Fogle, Walter E. Bezanson, Laurence Barrett, and Jack Capps.

Primary sources which have been especially helpful to me include Jay Leyda's *The Melville Log: A Documentary Life of Herman Melville 1819–1891* (New York: Harcourt, Brace and Company, 1951), Merton M. Sealts' *Melville as Lecturer* (Harvard University Press, 1957), *The Letters of Herman Melville*, edited by Merrell R. Davis and William H. Gilman (Yale University Press, 1960), and *Journal of a Visit to London and the Continent by Herman Melville: 1849–1850*, edited by Eleanor Melville Metcalfe (Harvard University Press, 1948).

H.C.

For M.L.C.
"One lonely good, let this but be!"
Melville's "L'Envoi"

Contents

Preface

The history of Herman Melville's literary reputation is somewhat curious. His short-sighted contemporaries, unable or unwilling to penetrate the depths of his art and ideas, saw him merely as a writer who had attained an early success for the description of his adventures in the South Seas; who appeared to falter for the moment when he sought to be pretentious and philosophical; who seemed on the way toward recovery with several other autobiographical stories of the sea; and who then perversely went off the track again, writing novels sodden with allegory and metaphysics. Nothing much was heard of him thereafter except that he composed some rough verses about the Civil War and a poem longer than *Paradise Lost* having to do with a group of eccentric travelers in the Holy Land who talk too much about science and religion, faith and doubt, the fall of man, the degradation of democratic dogma, and similar unpleasant subjects.

It is inaccurate to say that Melville was ever either totally ignored or entirely misunderstood, but it was not until the 1920s that he began to be appreciated widely. Nor is it enough to observe that today his literary reputation is secure, for this fails to indicate the degree of respect with which literary critics regard his writing or the meaningfulness it has for readers whose interest is private rather than professional. The evidence is convincing on both sides. On the one hand, the flood tide of scholarship has all but engulfed us and shows no signs of ebbing. On the other, Melville is being absorbed into the texture of our total existence in the way, at once superficial and profound, that is so characteristic of mass culture.

There remains, however, a facet of Melville's literary reputation that is still somewhat curious. A perceptive student of Melville, Willard Thorp, was sensitive to it when, in 1938, he raised the question: "What value can one put on Melville's poetry? Does the recent interest in its resurrection indicate that time may lift from it the pall of incomprehension, as *Moby-Dick* and *Pierre* have slowly won for themselves appreciative readers?" Today the prospects seem favorable. The pall is indeed being lifted, and evaluations are being made which indicate that further attention would be rewarding. In short, Melville the novelist has long since won acclaim; now Melville the poet is on his way toward a recognition that is overdue.

Herman Melville was born in New York City on August 1, 1819. His family was prosperous and well regarded. Allan Melville, his father, was a merchant with connections abroad, of British descent, of the Unitarian faith, and of a mercurial temperament. Maria Gansevoort, his mother, was of New York Dutch ancestry and a serious communicant of the Dutch Reformed Church. Allan Melville suffered financial reverses, and when he died in 1832 he left behind a wife, eight children, and his debts. That there were wealthy relatives made the family's genteel poverty even more uncomfortable. One result of his financial situation was that Herman Melville's education was not the best. Like Ishmael in *Moby-Dick*, he could say that "a whale-ship was my Yale College and my Harvard."

His "matriculation" took place in June 1839, when he signed on the packet *St. Lawrence*, bound for Liverpool. He returned to New York the following October, taught school for a season, visited an uncle in Illinois, and then on January 3, 1841, sailed from Fairhaven, Massachusetts, on the *Acushnet* for a whaling cruise in the Pacific. In July 1842, he and a companion jumped ship in the Marquesas Islands where he hid in the interior for a month. He then shipped on an Australian whaler, but at Tahiti, with several other rebellious sailors, refused duty and was imprisoned by the British Consul. He took this experience lightly, and by October he had slipped away to the nearby island of Eimeo. A month later he signed on a Nantucket whaler, served out the cruise, and was discharged at Honolulu. A summer of casual employment and beachcombing followed. In August he enlisted as an ordinary seaman on the frigate *United States.* Aboard the man-of-war he again visited the Marquesas and Tahiti as well as various Latin American ports. On October 14, 1844, Melville was discharged from the United States Navy at Boston. Shortly thereafter he was regaling his family with tales of his travels. By winter he had begun to write.

Typee (1846) and *Omoo* (1847), Melville's first two books, are factual accounts of personal experiences in the South Seas, whatever else they may also be as symbol, social criticism, or seedbed for techniques and ideas that flowered in later and greater works. They made Melville the bright young literary man of the season and encouraged him in the belief that he could live by his writing. He married Elizabeth Shaw at Boston and after a wedding trip to Canada set about establishing himself as a professional literary person in New York, with a degree of confidence and optimism that he was never again to show. *Mardi* (1849) begins in the vein of *Typee* and *Omoo*, realistically enough, aboard a whaler in the Pacific, but it ends in the realm of fantasy. A "chartless voyage," Melville had called it, and the reviewers expressed disappointment that he had chosen to sail among allegorical islands instead of the Marquesas. *Redburn* (1849) and *White-Jacket* (1850), again like *Typee* and *Omoo*, originate in Melville's own experiences. As is certainly to some degree in keeping with autobiographical fact, they are narratives of the initiation of young sailors into the world of manhood, an initiation which involves the discovery that things are not always what they seem on the surface and that conventional wisdom is not always as wise as it might first appear to be. *Redburn* has a telling subtitle: *His First Voyage. Being the Sailor-boy Confessions and Reminiscences of the Son-of-a-Gentleman, in the Merchant Service;* the subtitle of *White-Jacket* is equally significant: *The World in a Man-of-War.*

In 1851, at the height of his powers and with his apprenticeship behind him, Melville wrote *Moby-Dick.* What followed in the wake of this great whaling novel must inevitably seem anti-climactic but it would be incorrect to call it inferior. Melville was attempting other kinds of books, and comparison as a way of evaluation is not very profitable. He never ceased to seek new ways of seeing things and expressing himself, and when objects are designed by their creator to be different they cannot be treated as if they are the same.

Pierre, or the Ambiguities (1852) plunges deeply into the labyrinthian ways of the human soul, following threads left over from the "loomings" of *Moby-Dick*. The story of a young writer who destroyed himself and those about him through an attempt to live with rigorous honesty has its autobiographical ingredients also. *Israel Potter* (1855) and *The Piazza Tales* (1856), his next two books, are the work of a competent professional concerned with turning his talents to financial account, for by this time Melville had two sons and two daughters. First published as a magazine serial, *Israel Potter* is the rewriting of the autobiography of a Revolutionary War veteran who, after fifty years of misadventures abroad, made his way back to his native America. Melville transformed the crude account into a manual for survival based upon simple patience, good humor, and the knack of seeing and accepting things as they are. *The Piazza Tales*, likewise first written for magazine publication, contain examples of Melville's finest writing, including the existential fables "Bartleby," "Benito Cereno," and "The Encantadas." *The Confidence-Man* (1857), the last work of fiction published in his lifetime, is of still another variety. Set aboard a Mississippi River steamboat, it is a human comedy of self-deception.

Books like *Mardi*, *Pierre*, and *The Confidence-Man* were not calculated to attract readers in the expansive, optimistic 1850s, and Melville was incapable of shaping his output to the popular taste. His reaction was to withdraw. He had worked very hard, had written ten books in eleven years and some verse and reviews as well; he was no longer young, and his state of health was precarious. A tour of England and the Mediterranean was helpful. Upon his return he tried lecturing, with no great success.

In May 1860, Melville again embarked on a voyage, this time planning to sail from New York to San Francisco and thence to Manila aboard a merchant ship of which his brother, Thomas, was captain. He left behind a manuscript volume of poetry with instructions to his wife and his lawyer

brother, Allan, regarding its publication. On the trip around
Cape Horn he appears to have written other poems, some of
them harking back to his earlier experiences at sea. The voy-
age proved disappointing and he returned from San Fran-
cisco. At home he learned that a satisfactory publisher for
his verse could not be found.

For almost ten years Melville published nothing. In the
final days of the Civil War, moved by "an impulse imparted
by the fall of Richmond," if we are to accept his own words,
he began work on *Battle-Pieces*. He wrote rapidly; or for
that matter, considering the unevenness of the collection and
the discrepancies in quality within individual poems, per-
haps too rapidly. *Harper's New Monthly Magazine* pub-
lished five of them and Harper & Brothers, sensing the time-
liness of his subject and recalling his former popularity, and
—to do them justice—aware that the poems, though uncon-
ventional, had merit, brought out an edition of twelve hun-
dred copies in August 1866. The reviewers did not respond
with enthusiasm. In December, Melville became a customs
inspector for the Port of New York. Hawthorne, whom he
held in high esteem, filled a similar post *before* he became
a major literary figure, Melville, *after* he declined into ob-
scurity. But he had the consolation of contributing to the
welfare of his family, and he could write to please himself.
For the twenty-five years that remained to him he wrote
mainly verse and he published it privately.

There were three more books: the ambitious *Clarel* (1876),
in two volumes that Melville dutifully inscribed to his late
uncle, Peter Gansevoort, who had underwritten the printing
bill; *John Marr and Other Sailors* (1888), based principally
upon his memories of life as a seaman; and *Timoleon* (1891),
which recalls his actual travels to Europe, the Near East,
and the Pacific, and some imaginary voyaging as well. These
last two were each printed in neatly designed editions of
twenty-five copies, and Melville watched them carefully as
they went through the press. Now in retirement and finan-
cially independent through various legacies, he could indulge
himself in such ways. He also planned other volumes of
verse, drawing up title pages and making tentative selections.
One of these was a combination of prose and verse about a

convivial group that he called the "Burgundy Club." Another was a collection of deliberately unpretentious verse, dedicated to his beloved Elizabeth, that stemmed from their long residence in rural Pittsfield, Massachusetts, in the 1850s and early 60s. He planned to call it *Weeds and Wildings*, and he had a subsection titled "A Rose or Two." These two collections, a few miscellaneous poems, and the manuscript of his fine novella, *Billy Budd, Sailor*, were among his papers after he died on September 28, 1891.

In making the selections for this volume literary considerations were given the highest priority. Poems of lesser merit have also been included, however, because they show Melville's artistic development, the range of his ideas, or important relationships to his prose. Melville had his shortcomings as a poet. Technical polish was never one of his strong points, and his attempts to fill out a line or satisfy the demands of a rhyme pattern did not always succeed. But his failures were rarely those of the poetic imagination. The case should be stated positively. Melville in our time has emerged as an important poet for the power of his imagination, the integrity of his intellect, the scope of his interests, the depth of his courage, and the breadth of his human sympathies.

HENNIG COHEN
University of Pennsylvania
January 15, 1963

A Postscript

The original edition of *Selected Poems of Herman Melville* was put to press a generation ago. Since then the study of Melville and his writing has continued unabated, that of his verse included. Once looked upon as a curiosity, his poems appear routinely in the anthologies, and although he is not Walt Whitman or Emily Dickinson his place among the American poets of the nineteenth century is secure. Yet, for all of its attraction, his poetic achievement is not what primarily draws us to him. In this respect he is like his contemporaries, Emerson and Poe. We read their verse, and Melville's, within the contexts of their works as a whole. But when we read Melville's poetry, we find ourselves impressed by the space it occupies in his corpus—he published four volumes before his death and left much else behind—and by the space he gave it in his creative life. And although a number of his poems are trivial and flawed, a few are, within the scope of their intention, as flawless as anything he ever wrote.

Melville had less to say about his own writing than many authors, and he was especially reticent in reference to his poetry. *Clarel* he judged "eminently adapted for unpopularity," a verdict also applicable to his other poetry. He authorized the destruction of the unsold copies soon after publication, and subsequently published his poems privately. It was not popularity that he sought but understanding. He has found it in our time.

A new generation is reading Melville's poetry. It has the benefit of biographical information that should prove enlightening. For example, what do the recent discoveries regarding his estrangement from his wife and the suicide of his son in the 1860s (and his reconciliations) contribute to the making of his verse? It seems likely that further study of his family history will be helpful in this regard. Gender studies should provide us with richer readings of such a finely wrought poem as "The Marchioness of Brinvilliers" or such a passionate one as "After the Pleasure Party." And what will the New Historicism bring to "Formerly a Slave" or the well-known "A Utilitarian's View of the Monitor's Fight"? And there is still work to be done on Melville's experiments in form, such as "Tom Deadlight" and "John Marr." Finally, might it not be well to look back on the body of Melville's writing, as Melville did himself at the end of his life, and attend the consolation of Nature he heard in the song of the pines of "Pontoosuce"?

HENNIG COHEN
Swarthmore, Pennsylvania
February 1, 1991

The Civil War

THE PORTENT.

(1859.)

Hanging from the beam,
  Slowly swaying (such the law),
Gaunt the shadow on your green,
  Shenandoah!
The cut is on the crown
(Lo, John Brown),
And the stabs shall heal no more.

Hidden in the cap
  Is the anguish none can draw;
So your future veils its face,
  Shenandoah!
But the streaming beard is shown
(Weird John Brown),
The meteor of the war.

MISGIVINGS.

(1860.)

When ocean-clouds over inland hills
    Sweep storming in late autumn brown,
And horror the sodden valley fills,
    And the spire falls crashing in the town,
I muse upon my country's ills—
The tempest bursting from the waste of Time
On the world's fairest hope linked with man's foulest crime.

Nature's dark side is heeded now—
    (Ah! optimist-cheer disheartened flown)—
A child may read the moody brow
    Of yon black mountain lone.
With shouts the torrents down the gorges go,
    And storms are formed behind the storm we feel:
The hemlock shakes in the rafter, the oak in the driving keel.

THE CONFLICT OF CONVICTIONS.

(1860–1.)

On starry heights
  A bugle wails the long recall;
Derision stirs the deep abyss,
  Heaven's ominous silence over all.
Return, return, O eager Hope,
  And face man's latter fall.
Events, they make the dreamers quail;
Satan's old age is strong and hale,
A disciplined captain, gray in skill,
And Raphael a white enthusiast still;
Dashed aims, at which Christ's martyrs pale,
Shall Mammon's slaves fulfill?

> (*Dismantle the fort,*
> *Cut down the fleet—*
> *Battle no more shall be!*
> *While the fields for fight in æons to come*
> *Congeal beneath the sea.*)

The terrors of truth and dart of death
  To faith alike are vain;
Though comets, gone a thousand years,
    Return again,
Patient she stands—she can no more—
And waits, nor heeds she waxes hoar.

> (*At a stony gate,*
> *A statue of stone,*
> *Weed overgrown—*
> *Long 'twill wait!*)

But God his former mind retains,
  Confirms his old decree;
The generations are inured to pains,
  And strong Necessity

Surges, and heaps Time's strand with wrecks.
   The People spread like a weedy grass,
   The thing they will they bring to pass,
And prosper to the apoplex.
The rout it herds around the heart,
   The ghost is yielded in the gloom;
Kings wag their heads—Now save thyself
   Who wouldst rebuild the world in bloom.

      (Tide-mark
      And top of the ages' strife,
      Verge where they called the world to come,
      The last advance of life—
      Ha ha, the rust on the Iron Dome!)

Nay, but revere the hid event;
   In the cloud a sword is girded on,
I mark a twinkling in the tent
   Of Michael the warrior one.
Senior wisdom suits not now,
The light is on the youthful brow.

      (Ay, in caves the miner see:
      His forehead bears a blinking light;
      Darkness so he feebly braves—
      A meagre wight!)

But He who rules is old—is old;
Ah! faith is warm, but heaven with age is cold.

      (Ho ho, ho ho,
      The cloistered doubt
      Of olden times
      Is blurted out!)

The Ancient of Days forever is young,
   Forever the scheme of Nature thrives;
I know a wind in purpose strong—
   It spins *against* the way it drives.

What if the gulfs their slimed foundations bare?
So deep must the stones be hurled
Whereon the throes of ages rear
The final empire and the happier world.

> (*The poor old Past,*
> *The Future's slave,*
> *She drudged through pain and crime*
> *To bring about the blissful Prime,*
> *Then—perished.* There's *a grave!*)

  Power unanointed may come—
Dominion(unsought by the free)
  And the Iron Dome,
Stronger for stress and strain,
Fling her huge shadow athwart the main;
But the Founders' dream shall flee.
Age after age shall be
As age after age has been,
(From man's changeless heart their way they win);
And death be busy with all who strive—
Death, with silent negative.

> YEA AND NAY—
> EACH HATH HIS SAY;
> BUT GOD HE KEEPS THE MIDDLE WAY.
> NONE WAS BY
> WHEN HE SPREAD THE SKY;
> WISDOM IS VAIN, AND PROPHESY.

APATHY AND ENTHUSIASM.
(1860–1.)

I.

O the clammy cold November,
    And the winter white and dead,
And the terror dumb with stupor,
    And the sky a sheet of lead;
And events that came resounding
    With the cry that *All was lost,*
Like the thunder-cracks of massy ice
    In intensity of frost—
Bursting one upon another
    Through the horror of the calm.
    The paralysis of arm
In the anguish of the heart;
And the hollowness and dearth.
    The appealings of the mother
    To brother and to brother
Not in hatred so to part—
And the fissure in the hearth
    Growing momently more wide.
Then the glances 'tween the Fates,
    And the doubt on every side,
And the patience under gloom
In the stoniness that waits
The finality of doom.

II.

So the winter died despairing,
    And the weary weeks of Lent;
And the ice-bound rivers melted,
    And the tomb of Faith was rent.

O, the rising of the People
    Came with springing of the grass,
They rebounded from dejection
    After Easter came to pass.
And the young were all elation
    Hearing Sumter's cannon roar,
And they thought how tame the Nation
    In the age that went before.
And Michael seemed gigantical,
    The Arch-fiend but a dwarf:
And at the towers of Erebus
    Our striplings flung the scoff.
But the elders with foreboding
    Mourned the days forever o'er,
And recalled the forest proverb,
    The Iroquois' old saw:
Grief to every graybeard
    When young Indians lead the war.

THE MARCH INTO VIRGINIA,

Ending in the First Manassas.

(JULY, 1861.)

Did all the lets and bars appear
   To every just or larger end,
Whence should come the trust and cheer?
   Youth must its ignorant impulse lend—
Age finds place in the rear.
   All wars are boyish, and are fought by boys,
The champions and enthusiasts of the state:
   Turbid ardors and vain joys
     Not barrenly abate—
   Stimulants to the power mature,
     Preparatives of fate.

Who here forecasteth the event?
What heart but spurns at precedent
And warnings of the wise,
Contemned foreclosures of surprise?
The banners play, the bugles call,
The air is blue and prodigal.
   No berrying party, pleasure-wooed,
No picnic party in the May,
Ever went less loth than they
   Into that leafy neighborhood.
In Bacchic glee they file toward Fate,
Moloch's uninitiate;
Expectancy, and glad surmise
Of battle's unknown mysteries.
All they feel is this: 'tis glory,
A rapture sharp, though transitory,
Yet lasting in belaureled story.
So they gayly go to fight,
Chatting left and laughing right.

But some who this blithe mood present,
    As on in lightsome files they fare,
Shall die experienced ere three days are spent—
    Perish, enlightened by the vollied glare;
Or shame survive, and, like to adamant,
    The throe of Second Manassas share.

BALL'S BLUFF.

A *Reverie.*

(OCTOBER, 1861.)

One noonday, at my window in the town,
   I saw a sight—saddest that eyes can see—
   Young soldiers marching lustily
      Unto the wars,
With fifes, and flags in mottoed pageantry;
     While all the porches, walks, and doors
Were rich with ladies cheering royally.

They moved like Juny morning on the wave,
   Their hearts were fresh as clover in its prime
   (It was the breezy summer time),
      Life throbbed so strong,
How should they dream that Death in a rosy clime
     Would come to thin their shining throng?
Youth feels immortal, like the gods sublime.

Weeks passed; and at my window, leaving bed,
   By night I mused, of easeful sleep bereft,
   On those brave boys (Ah War! thy theft);
      Some marching feet
Found pause at last by cliffs Potomac cleft;
     Wakeful I mused, while in the street
Far footfalls died away till none were left.

DUPONT'S ROUND FIGHT.

(NOVEMBER, 1861.)

In time and measure perfect moves
    All Art whose aim is sure;
Evolving rhyme and stars divine
    Have rules, and they endure.

Nor less the Fleet that warred for Right,
    And, warring so, prevailed,
In geometric beauty curved,
    And in an orbit sailed.

The rebel at Port Royal felt
    The Unity overawe,
And rued the spell. A type was here,
    And victory of Law.

IN THE TURRET.

(MARCH, 1862.)

Your honest heart of duty, Worden,
　　So helped you that in fame you dwell;
You bore the first iron battle's burden
　　Sealed as in a diving-bell.
Alcides, groping into haunted hell
To bring forth King Admetus' bride,
Braved naught more vaguely direful and untried.
　　What poet shall uplift his charm,
Bold Sailor, to your height of daring,
　　And interblend therewith the calm,
And build a goodly style upon your bearing.

Escaped the gale of outer ocean—
　　Cribbed in a craft which like a log
Was washed by every billow's motion—
　　By night you heard of Og
The huge; nor felt your courage clog
At tokens of his onset grim:
You marked the sunk ship's flag-staff slim,
　　Lit by her burning sister's heart;
You marked, and mused: "Day brings the trial:
　　Then be it proved if I have part
With men whose manhood never took denial."

A prayer went up—a champion's. Morning
　　Beheld you in the Turret walled
By adamant, where a spirit forewarning
　　And all-deriding called:
"Man, darest thou—desperate, unappalled—
Be first to lock thee in the armored tower?
I have thee now; and what the battle-hour
　　To me shall bring—heed well—thou'lt share;
This plot-work, planned to be the foeman's terror,
　　To thee may prove a goblin-snare;
Its very strength and cunning—monstrous error!"

"Stand up, my heart; be strong; what matter
    If here thou seest thy welded tomb?
And let huge Og with thunders batter—
    Duty be still my doom,
Though drowning come in liquid gloom;
First duty, duty next, and duty last;
Ay, Turret, rivet me here to duty fast!"—
    So nerved, you fought, wisely and well;
And live, twice live in life and story;
    But over your Monitor dirges swell,
In wind and wave that keep the rites of glory.

THE TEMERAIRE.

(Supposed to have been suggested to an Englishman of the old order by the fight of the Monitor and Merrimac.)

The gloomy hulls, in armor grim,
　　Like clouds o'er moors have met,
And prove that oak, and iron, and man
　　Are tough in fibre yet.

But Splendors wane. The sea-fight yields
　　No front of old display;
The garniture, emblazonment,
　　And heraldry all decay.

Towering afar in parting light,
　　The fleets like Albion's forelands shine—
The full-sailed fleets, the shrouded show
　　Of Ships-of-the-Line.

The fighting Temeraire,
　　Built of a thousand trees,
Lunging out her lightnings,
　　And beetling o'er the seas—
O Ship, how brave and fair,
　　That fought so oft and well,
On open decks you manned the gun
　　　　Armorial.
What cheerings did you share,
　　Impulsive in the van,
When down upon leagued France and Spain
　　We English ran—
The freshet at your bowsprit
　　Like the foam upon the can.
Bickering, your colors
　　Licked up the Spanish air,
You flapped with flames of battle-flags—
　　Your challenge, Temeraire!

The rear ones of our fleet
  They yearned to share your place,
Still vying with the Victory
  Throughout that earnest race—
The Victory, whose Admiral,
  With orders nobly won,
Shone in the globe of the battle glow—
  The angel in that sun.

Parallel in story,
  Lo, the stately pair,
As late in grapple ranging,
  The foe between them there—
When four great hulls lay tiered,
And the fiery tempest cleared,
And your prizes twain appeared,
        Temeraire!

But Trafalgar' is over now,
  The quarter-deck undone;
The carved and castled navies fire
  Their evening-gun.
O, Titan Temeraire,
  Your stern-lights fade away;
Your bulwarks to the years must yield,
  And heart-of-oak decay.
A pigmy steam-tug tows you,
  Gigantic, to the shore—
Dismantled of your guns and spars,
  And sweeping wings of war.
The rivets clinch the iron-clads,
  Men learn a deadlier lore;
But Fame has nailed your battle-flags—
  Your ghost it sails before:
O, the navies old and oaken,
  O, the Temeraire no more!

A UTILITARIAN VIEW OF THE MONITOR'S FIGHT.

Plain be the phrase, yet apt the verse,
   More ponderous than nimble;
For since grimed War here laid aside
His Orient pomp, 'twould ill befit
     Overmuch to ply
   The rhyme's barbaric cymbal.

Hail to victory without the gaud
   Of glory; zeal that needs no fans
Of banners; plain mechanic power
Plied cogently in War now placed—
     Where War belongs—
   Among the trades and artisans.

Yet this was battle, and intense—
   Beyond the strife of fleets heroic;
Deadlier, closer, calm 'mid storm;
No passion; all went on by crank,
     Pivot, and screw,
   And calculations of caloric.

Needless to dwell; the story's known.
   The ringing of those plates on plates
Still ringeth round the world—
The clangor of that blacksmiths' fray.
     The anvil-din
   Resounds this message from the Fates:

War shall yet be, and to the end;
   But war-paint shows the streaks of weather;
War yet shall be, but warriors
Are now but operatives; War's made
     Less grand than Peace,
   And a singe runs through lace and feather.

SHILOH.

A *Requiem*.

(APRIL, 1862.)

Skimming lightly, wheeling still,
    The swallows fly low
Over the field in clouded days,
    The forest-field of Shiloh—
Over the field where April rain
Solaced the parched ones stretched in pain
Through the pause of night
That followed the Sunday fight
    Around the church of Shiloh—
The church so lone, the log-built one,
That echoed to many a parting groan
        And natural prayer
Of dying foemen mingled there—
Foemen at morn, but friends at eve—
    Fame or country least their care:
(What like a bullet can undeceive!)
    But now they lie low,
While over them the swallows skim,
    And all is hushed at Shiloh.

MALVERN HILL.

(JULY, 1862.)

Ye elms that wave on Malvern Hill
  In prime of morn and May,
Recall ye how McClellan's men
    Here stood at bay?
While deep within yon forest dim
  Our rigid comrades lay—
Some with the cartridge in their mouth,
Others with fixed arms lifted South—
    Invoking so
The cypress glades? Ah wilds of woe!

The spires of Richmond, late beheld
  Through rifts in musket-haze,
Were closed from view in clouds of dust
  On leaf-walled ways,
Where streamed our wagons in caravan;
  And the Seven Nights and Days
Of march and fast, retreat and fight,
Pinched our grimed faces to ghastly plight—
    Does the elm wood
Recall the haggard beards of blood?

The battle-smoked flag, with stars eclipsed,
  We followed (it never fell!)—
In silence husbanded our strength—
    Received their yell;
Till on this slope we patient turned
  With cannon ordered well;
Reverse we proved was not defeat;
But ah, the sod what thousands meet!—
    Does Malvern Wood
Bethink itself, and muse and brood?

We elms of Malvern Hill
  Remember every thing;
But sap the twig will fill:
Wag the world how it will,
  Leaves must be green in Spring.

BATTLE OF STONE RIVER, TENNESSEE.

A View from Oxford Cloisters.

(JANUARY, 1863.)

With Tewksbury and Barnet heath
  In days to come the field shall blend,
The story dim and date obscure;
  In legend all shall end.
Even now, involved in forest shade
  A Druid-dream the strife appears,
The fray of yesterday assumes
    The haziness of years.
        In North and South still beats the vein
        Of Yorkist and Lancastrian.

Our rival Roses warred for Sway—
  For Sway, but named the name of Right;
And Passion, scorning pain and death,
  Lent sacred fervor to the fight.
Each lifted up a broidered cross,
  While crossing blades profaned the sign;
Monks blessed the fratricidal lance,
  And sisters scarfs could twine.
        Do North and South the sin retain
        Of Yorkist and Lancastrian?

But Rosecrans in the cedarn glade,
  And, deep in denser cypress gloom,
Dark Breckinridge, shall fade away
    Or thinly loom.
The pale throngs who in forest cowed
  Before the spell of battle's pause,
Forefelt the stillness that shall dwell
  On them and on their wars.
        North and South shall join the train
        Of Yorkist and Lancastrian.

But where the sword has plunged so deep,
  And then been turned within the wound
By deadly Hate; where Climes contend
    On vasty ground—
No warning Alps or seas between,
  And small the curb of creed or law,
And blood is quick, and quick the brain;
  Shall North and South their rage deplore,
    And reunited thrive amain
    Like Yorkist and Lancastrian?

STONEWALL JACKSON.

Mortally wounded at Chancellorsville.

(MAY, 1863.)

The Man who fiercest charged in fight,
   Whose sword and prayer were long—
         Stonewall!
   Even him who stoutly stood for Wrong,
How can we praise? Yet coming days
   Shall not forget him with this song.

Dead is the Man whose Cause is dead,
   Vainly he died and set his seal—
         Stonewall!
   Earnest in error, as we feel;
True to the thing he deemed was due,
   True as John Brown or steel.

Relentlessly he routed us;
   But *we* relent, for he is low—
         Stonewall!
   Justly his fame we outlaw; so
We drop a tear on the bold Virginian's bier,
   Because no wreath we owe.

THE HOUSE-TOP.

A *Night Piece.*

(JULY, 1863.)

No sleep. The sultriness pervades the air
And binds the brain—a dense oppression, such
As tawny tigers feel in matted shades,
Vexing their blood and making apt for ravage.
Beneath the stars the roofy desert spreads
Vacant as Libya. All is hushed near by.
Yet fitfully from far breaks a mixed surf
Of muffled sound, the Atheist roar of riot.
Yonder, where parching Sirius set in drought,
Balefully glares red Arson—there—and there.
The Town is taken by its rats—ship-rats
And rats of the wharves. All civil charms
And priestly spells which late held hearts in awe—
Fear-bound, subjected to a better sway
Than sway of self; these like a dream dissolve,
And man rebounds whole æons back in nature.
Hail to the low dull rumble, dull and dead,
And ponderous drag that shakes the wall.
Wise Draco comes, deep in the midnight roll
Of black artillery; he comes, though late;
In code corroborating Calvin's creed
And cynic tyrannies of honest kings;
He comes, nor parlies; and the Town, redeemed,
Gives thanks devout; nor, being thankful, heeds
The grimy slur on the Republic's faith implied,
Which holds that Man is naturally good,
And—more—is Nature's Roman, never to be scourged.

THE ARMIES OF THE WILDERNESS.

(1863–4.)

I.

Like snows the camps on Southern hills
  Lay all the winter long,
Our levies there in patience stood—
  They stood in patience strong.
On fronting slopes gleamed other camps
  Where faith as firmly clung:
Ah, froward kin! so brave amiss—
  The zealots of the Wrong.

> *In this strife of brothers*
>   *(God, hear their country call),*
> *However it be, whatever betide,*
>   *Let not the just one fall.*

Through the pointed glass our soldiers saw
  The base-ball bounding sent;
They could have joined them in their sport
  But for the vale's deep rent.
And others turned the reddish soil,
  Like diggers of graves they bent:
The reddish soil and trenching toil
    Begat presentiment.

> *Did the Fathers feel mistrust?*
>   *Can no final good be wrought?*
> *Over and over, again and again*
>   *Must the fight for the Right be fought?*

They lead a Gray-back to the crag:
  "Your earth-works yonder—tell us, man!"
"A prisoner—no deserter, I,
  Nor one of the tell-tale clan."

His rags they mark: "True-blue like you
  Should wear the color—your Country's, man!"
He grinds his teeth: "However that be,
  Yon earth-works have their plan."

> *Such brave ones, foully snared*
>   *By Belial's wily plea,*
> *Were faithful unto the evil end—*
>   *Feudal fidelity.*

"Well, then, your camps—come, tell the names!"
  Freely he leveled his finger then:
"Yonder—see—are our Georgians; on the crest,
  The Carolinians; lower, past the glen,
Virginians—Alabamians—Mississippians—Kentuckians
  (Follow my finger)—Tennesseeans; and the ten
Camps *there*—ask your grave-pits; they'll tell.
  Halloa! I see the picket-hut, the den
Where I last night lay." "Where's Lee?"
  "In the hearts and bayonets of all yon men!"

> *The tribes swarm up to war*
>   *As in ages long ago,*
> *Ere the palm of promise leaved*
>   *And the lily of Christ did blow.*

Their mounted pickets for miles are spied
  Dotting the lowland plain,
The nearer ones in their veteran-rags—
  Loutish they loll in lazy disdain.
But ours in perilous places bide
  With rifles ready and eyes that strain
Deep through the dim suspected wood
  Where the Rapidan rolls amain.

> *The Indian has passed away,*
>   *But creeping comes another—*
> *Deadlier far. Picket,*
>   *Take heed—take heed of thy brother!*

From a wood-hung height, an outpost lone,
  Crowned with a woodman's fort,
The sentinel looks on a land of dole,
    Like Paran, all amort.
Black chimneys, gigantic in moor-like wastes,
  The scowl of the clouded sky retort;
The hearth is a houseless stone again—
  Ah! where shall the people be sought?

> *Since the venom such blastment deals,*
>   *The South should have paused, and thrice,*
> *Ere with heat of her hate she hatched*
>   *The egg with the cockatrice.*

A path down the mountain winds to the glade
  Where the dead of the Moonlight Fight lie low;
A hand reaches out of the thin-laid mould
  As begging help which none can bestow.
But the field-mouse small and busy ant
  Heap their hillocks, to hide if they may the woe:
By the bubbling spring lies the rusted canteen,
  And the drum which the drummer-boy dying let go.

> *Dust to dust, and blood for blood—*
> *Passion and pangs! Has Time*
> *Gone back? or is this the Age*
> *Of the world's great Prime?*

The wagon mired and cannon dragged
  Have trenched their scar; the plain
Tramped like the cindery beach of the damned—
  A site for the city of Cain.
And stumps of forests for dreary leagues
  Like a massacre show. The armies have lain
By fires where gums and balms did burn,
  And the seeds of Summer's reign.

> *Where are the birds and boys?*
> *Who shall go chestnutting when*
> *October returns? The nuts—*
>   *O, long ere they grow again.*

They snug their huts with the chapel-pews,
  In court-houses stable their steeds—
Kindle their fires with indentures and bonds,
  And old Lord Fairfax's parchment deeds;
And Virginian gentlemen's libraries old—
  Books which only the scholar heeds—
Are flung to his kennel. It is ravage and range,
  And gardens are left to weeds.

> *Turned adrift into war*
>   *Man runs wild on the plain,*
> *Like the jennets let loose*
>   *On the Pampas—zebras again.*

Like the Pleiads dim, see the tents through the storm—
  Aloft by the hill-side hamlet's graves,
On a head-stone used for a hearth-stone there
  The water is bubbling for punch for our braves.
What if the night be drear, and the blast
  Ghostly shrieks? their rollicking staves
Make frolic the heart; beating time with their swords,
  What care they if Winter raves?

> *Is life but a dream? and so,*
>   *In the dream do men laugh aloud?*
> *So strange seems mirth in a camp,*
>   *So like a white tent to a shroud.*

II.

The May-weed springs; and comes a Man
  And mounts our Signal Hill;
A quiet Man, and plain in garb—
  Briefly he looks his fill,
Then drops his gray eye on the ground,
  Like a loaded mortar he is still:
Meekness and grimness meet in him—
  The silent General.

Were men but strong and wise,
Honest as Grant, and calm,
War would be left to the red and black ants,
And the happy world disarm.

That eve a stir was in the camps,
  Forerunning quiet soon to come
Among the streets of beechen huts
  No more to know the drum.
The weed shall choke the lowly door,
  And foxes peer within the gloom,
Till scared perchance by Mosby's prowling men,
  Who ride in the rear of doom.

Far West, and farther South,
  Wherever the sword has been,
Deserted camps are met,
  And desert graves are seen.

The livelong night they ford the flood;
  With guns held high they silent press,
Till shimmers the grass in their bayonets' sheen—
  On Morning's banks their ranks they dress;
Then by the forests lightly wind,
  Whose waving boughs the pennons seem to bless,
Borne by the cavalry scouting on—
  Sounding the Wilderness.

Like shoals of fish in spring
  That visit Crusoe's isle,
The host in the lonesome place—
  The hundred thousand file.

The foe that held his guarded hills
  Must speed to woods afar;
For the scheme that was nursed by the Culpeper hearth
  With the slowly-smoked cigar—
The scheme that smouldered through winter long
  Now bursts into act—into war—
The resolute scheme of a heart as calm
  As the Cyclone's core.

> *The fight for the city is fought*
> *In Nature's old domain;*
> *Man goes out to the wilds,*
> *And Orpheus' charm is vain.*

In glades they meet skull after skull
  Where pine-cones lay—the rusted gun,
Green shoes full of bones, the mouldering coat
  And cuddled-up skeleton;
And scores of such. Some start as in dreams,
  And comrades lost bemoan:
By the edge of those wilds Stonewall had charged—
  But the Year and the Man were gone.

> *At the height of their madness*
> *The night winds pause,*
> *Recollecting themselves;*
> *But no lull in these wars.*

A gleam!—a volley! And who shall go
  Storming the swarmers in jungles dread?
No cannon-ball answers, no proxies are sent—
  They rush in the shrapnel's stead.
Plume and sash are vanities now—
  Let them deck the pall of the dead;
They go where the shade is, perhaps into Hades,
  Where the brave of all times have led.

> *There's a dust of hurrying feet,*
> *Bitten lips and bated breath,*
> *And drums that challenge to the grave,*
> *And faces fixed, forefeeling death.*

What husky huzzahs in the hazy groves—
  What flying encounters fell;
Pursuer and pursued like ghosts disappear
  In gloomed shade—their end who shall tell?
The crippled, a ragged-barked stick for a crutch,
  Limp to some elfin dell—
Hobble from the sight of dead faces—white
  As pebbles in a well.

Few burial rites shall be;
No priest with book and band
Shall come to the secret place
Of the corpse in the foeman's land.

Watch and fast, march and fight—clutch your gun!
Day-fights and night-fights; sore is the stress;
Look, through the pines what line comes on?
Longstreet slants through the hauntedness!
'Tis charge for charge, and shout for yell:
Such battles on battles oppress—
But Heaven lent strength, the Right strove well,
And emerged from the Wilderness.

Emerged, for the way was won;
But the Pillar of Smoke that led
Was brand-like with ghosts that went up
Ashy and red.

None can narrate that strife in the pines,
A seal is on it—Sabæan lore!
Obscure as the wood, the entangled rhyme
But hints at the maze of war—
Vivid glimpses or livid through peopled gloom,
And fires which creep and char—
A riddle of death, of which the slain
Sole solvers are.

Long they withhold the roll
Of the shroudless dead. It is right;
Not yet can we bear the flare
Of the funeral light.

ON THE PHOTOGRAPH OF A CORPS COMMANDER.

Ay, man is manly. Here you see
  The warrior-carriage of the head,
And brave dilation of the frame;
  And lighting all, the soul that led
In Spottsylvania's charge to victory,
  Which justifies his fame.

A cheering picture. It is good
  To look upon a Chief like this,
In whom the spirit moulds the form.
  Here favoring Nature, oft remiss,
With eagle mien expressive has endued
  A man to kindle strains that warm.

Trace back his lineage, and his sires,
  Yeoman or noble, you shall find
Enrolled with men of Agincourt,
  Heroes who shared great Harry's mind.
Down to us come the knightly Norman fires,
  And front the Templars bore.

Nothing can lift the heart of man
  Like manhood in a fellow-man.
The thought of heaven's great King afar
  But humbles us—too weak to scan;
But manly greatness men can span,
  And feel the bonds that draw.

SHERIDAN AT CEDAR CREEK.

(OCTOBER, 1864.)

Shoe the steed with silver
  That bore him to the fray,
When he heard the guns at dawning—
      Miles away;
When he heard them calling, calling—
      Mount! nor stay:
         Quick, or all is lost;
         They've surprised and stormed the post,
         They push your routed host—
  Gallop! retrieve the day.

House the horse in ermine—
  For the foam-flake blew
White through the red October;
  He thundered into view;
They cheered him in the looming,
  Horseman and horse they knew.
         The turn of the tide began,
         The rally of bugles ran,
         He swung his hat in the van;
  The electric hoof-spark flew.

Wreathe the steed and lead him—
  For the charge he led
Touched and turned the cypress
  Into amaranths for the head
Of Philip, king of riders,
  Who raised them from the dead.
         The camp (at dawning lost),
         By eve, recovered—forced,
         Rang with laughter of the host
  At belated Early fled.

Shroud the horse in sable—
  For the mounds they heap!
There is firing in the Valley,
  And yet no strife they keep;
It is the parting volley,
  It is the pathos deep.
        There is glory for the brave
        Who lead, and nobly save,
        But no knowledge in the grave
Where the nameless followers sleep.

THE COLLEGE COLONEL.

He rides at their head;
    A crutch by his saddle just slants in view,
One slung arm is in splints, you see,
    Yet he guides his strong steed—how coldly too.

He brings his regiment home—
    Not as they filed two years before,
But a remnant half-tattered, and battered, and worn,
Like castaway sailors, who—stunned
        By the surf's loud roar,
    Their mates dragged back and seen no more—
Again and again breast the surge,
    And at last crawl, spent, to shore.

A still rigidity and pale—
    An Indian aloofness lones his brow;
He has lived a thousand years
Compressed in battle's pains and prayers,
    Marches and watches slow.

There are welcoming shouts, and flags;
    Old men off hat to the Boy,
Wreaths from gay balconies fall at his feet,
    But to *him*—there comes alloy.

It is not that a leg is lost,
    It is not that an arm is maimed,
It is not that the fever has racked—
    Self he has long disclaimed.

But all through the Seven Days' Fight,
    And deep in the Wilderness grim,
And in the field-hospital tent,
    And Petersburg crater, and dim
Lean brooding in Libby, there came—
    Ah heaven!—what *truth* to him.

AT THE CANNON'S MOUTH.

Destruction of the Ram Albemarle by the Torpedo-launch.

(OCTOBER, 1864.)

Palely intent, he urged his keel
  Full on the guns, and touched the spring;
Himself involved in the bolt he drove
Timed with the armed hull's shot that stove
His shallop—die or do!
Into the flood his life he threw,
  Yet lives—unscathed—a breathing thing
To marvel at.

                    He has his fame;
But that mad dash at death, how name?

Had Earth no charm to stay the Boy
  From the martyr-passion? Could he dare
Disdain the Paradise of opening joy
  Which beckons the fresh heart every where?
Life has more lures than any girl
  For youth and strength; puts forth a share
Of beauty, hinting of yet rarer store;
And ever with unfathomable eyes,
        Which bafflingly entice,
Still strangely does Adonis draw.
And life once over, who shall tell the rest?
Life is, of all we know, God's best.
What imps these eagles then, that they
Fling disrespect on life by that proud way
In which they soar above our lower clay.

Pretense of wonderment and doubt unblest:
  In Cushing's eager deed was shown
  A spirit which brave poets own—
That scorn of life which earns life's crown;
  Earns, but not always wins; but *he*—
  The star ascended in his nativity.

THE MARCH TO THE SEA.

(DECEMBER, 1864.)

Not Kenesaw high-arching,
  Not Allatoona's glen—
Though there the graves lie parching—
  Stayed Sherman's miles of men;
From charred Atlanta marching
  They launched the sword again.
      The columns streamed like rivers
        Which in their course agree,
      And they streamed until their flashing
        Met the flashing of the sea:
          It was glorious glad marching,
          That marching to the sea.

They brushed the foe before them
  (Shall gnats impede the bull?);
Their own good bridges bore them
  Over swamps or torrents full,
And the grand pines waving o'er them
  Bowed to axes keen and cool.
      The columns grooved their channels,
        Enforced their own decree,
      And their power met nothing larger
        Until it met the sea:
          It was glorious glad marching,
          A marching glad and free.

Kilpatrick's snare of riders
  In zigzags mazed the land,
Perplexed the pale Southsiders
  With feints on every hand;
Vague menace awed the hiders
  In forts beyond command.

To Sherman's shifting problem
No foeman knew the key;
But onward went the marching
Unpausing to the sea:
It was glorious glad marching,
The swinging step was free.

The flankers ranged like pigeons
In clouds through field or wood;
The flocks of all those regions,
The herds and horses good,
Poured in and swelled the legions,
For they caught the marching mood.
A volley ahead! They hear it;
And they hear the repartee:
Fighting was but frolic
In that marching to the sea:
It was glorious glad marching,
A marching bold and free.

All nature felt their coming,
The birds like couriers flew,
And the banners brightly blooming
The slaves by thousands drew,
And they marched beside the drumming,
And they joined the armies blue.
The cocks crowed from the cannon
(Pets named from Grant and Lee),
Plumed fighters and campaigners
In that marching to the sea:
It was glorious glad marching,
For every man was free.

The foragers through calm lands
Swept in tempest gay,
And they breathed the air of balm-lands
Where rolled savannas lay,
And they helped themselves from farm-lands—

As who should say them nay?
　　The regiments uproarious
　　　Laughed in Plenty's glee;
　And they marched till their broad laughter
　　Met the laughter of the sea:
　　　　It was glorious glad marching,
　　　　That marching to the sea.

The grain of endless acres
　Was threshed (as in the East)
By the trampling of the Takers,
　Strong march of man and beast;
The flails of those earth-shakers
　Left a famine where they ceased.
　　　The arsenals were yielded;
　　　　The sword (that was to be),
　　Arrested in the forging,
　　　Rued that marching to the sea:
　　　　　It was glorious glad marching,
　　　　　But ah, the stern decree!

For behind they left a wailing,
　A terror and a ban,
And blazing cinders sailing,
　And houseless households wan,
Wide zones of counties paling,
　And towns where maniacs ran.
　　　Was it Treason's retribution—
　　　Necessity the plea?
　　They will long remember Sherman
　　　And his streaming columns free—
　　　　They will long remember Sherman
　　　　Marching to the sea.

A CANTICLE:

*Significant of the national exaltation of enthusiasm at
the close of the War.*

O the precipice Titanic
  Of the congregated Fall,
And the angle oceanic
  Where the deepening thunders call—
    And the Gorge so grim,
    And the firmamental rim!
Multitudinously thronging
  The waters all converge,
Then they sweep adown in sloping
  Solidity of surge.

      The Nation, in her impulse
        Mysterious as the Tide,
     In emotion like an ocean
       Moves in power, not in pride;
     And is deep in her devotion
       As Humanity is wide.

          Thou Lord of hosts victorious,
           The confluence Thou hast twined;
          By a wondrous way and glorious
           A passage Thou dost find—
           A passage Thou dost find:
          Hosanna to the Lord of hosts,
           The hosts of human kind.

Stable in its baselessness
  When calm is in the air,
The Iris half in tracelessness
  Hovers faintly fair.
Fitfully assailing it
  A wind from heaven blows,
Shivering and paling it
  To blankness of the snows;

While, incessant in renewal,
   The Arch rekindled grows,
Till again the gem and jewel
   Whirl in blinding overthrows—
Till, prevailing and transcending,
   Lo, the Glory perfect there,
And the contest finds an ending,
   For repose is in the air.

But the foamy Deep unsounded,
   And the dim and dizzy ledge,
And the booming roar rebounded,
   And the gull that skims the edge!
      The Giant of the Pool
      Heaves his forehead white as wool—
Toward the Iris ever climbing
   From the Cataracts that call—
Irremovable vast arras
   Draping all the Wall.

      The Generations pouring
         From times of endless date,
      In their going, in their flowing
         Ever form the steadfast State;
      And Humanity is growing
         Toward the fullness of her fate.

         Thou Lord of hosts victorious,
           Fulfill the end designed;
         By a wondrous way and glorious
           A passage Thou dost find—
           A passage Thou dost find:
         Hosanna to the Lord of hosts,
           The hosts of human kind.

THE MARTYR.

Indicative of the passion of the people on the 15th of April, 1865.

Good Friday was the day
  Of the prodigy and crime,
When they killed him in his pity,
  When they killed him in his prime
Of clemency and calm—
    When with yearning he was filled
    To redeem the evil-willed,
And, though conqueror, be kind;
  But they killed him in his kindness,
  In their madness and their blindness,
And they killed him from behind.

          There is sobbing of the strong,
            And a pall upon the land;
          But the People in their weeping
                Bare the iron hand:
          Beware the People weeping
            When they bare the iron hand.

He lieth in his blood—
  The father in his face;
They have killed him, the Forgiver—
  The Avenger takes his place,
The Avenger wisely stern,
    Who in righteousness shall do
    What the heavens call him to,
And the parricides remand;
  For they killed him in his kindness,
  In their madness and their blindness,
And his blood is on their hand.

There is sobbing of the strong,
　　And a pall upon the land;
But the People in their weeping
　　　　Bare the iron hand:
Beware the People weeping
　　When they bare the iron hand.

"THE COMING STORM:"

*A Picture by S. R. Gifford, and owned by E. B. Included
in the N. A. Exhibition, April,* 1865.

All feeling hearts must feel for him
    Who felt this picture. Presage dim—
Dim inklings from the shadowy sphere
    Fixed him and fascinated here.

A demon-cloud like the mountain one
    Burst on a spirit as mild
As this urned lake, the home of shades.
    But Shakspeare's pensive child

Never the lines had lightly scanned,
    Steeped in fable, steeped in fate;
The Hamlet in his heart was 'ware,
    Such hearts can antedate.

No utter surprise can come to him
    Who reaches Shakspeare's core;
That which we seek and shun is there—
    Man's final lore.

REBEL COLOR-BEARERS AT SHILOH:

A plea against the vindictive cry raised by civilians
shortly after the surrender at Appomattox.

The color-bearers facing death
White in the whirling sulphurous wreath,
　　Stand boldly out before the line;
Right and left their glances go,
Proud of each other, glorying in their show;
Their battle-flags about them blow,
　　And fold them as in flame divine:
Such living robes are only seen
Round martyrs burning on the green—
And martyrs for the Wrong have been.

Perish their Cause! but mark the men—
Mark the planted statues, then
Draw trigger on them if you can.

The leader of a patriot-band
Even so could view rebels who so could stand;
　　And this when peril pressed him sore,
Left aidless in the shivered front of war—
　　Skulkers behind, defiant foes before,
And fighting with a broken brand.
The challenge in that courage rare—
Courage defenseless, proudly bare—
Never could tempt him; he could dare
Strike up the leveled rifle there.

Sunday at Shiloh, and the day
When Stonewall charged—McClellan's crimson May,
And Chickamauga's wave of death,
And of the Wilderness the cypress wreath—
　　All these have passed away.

The life in the veins of Treason lags,
Her daring color-bearers drop their flags,
    And yield. *Now* shall we fire?
        Can poor spite be?
Shall nobleness in victory less aspire
Than in reverse? Spare Spleen her ire,
    And think how Grant met Lee.

THE MUSTER:

Suggested by the Two Days' Review at Washington.

(MAY, 1865.)

The Abrahamic river—
Patriarch of floods,
Calls the roll of all his streams
And watery multitudes:
> Torrent cries to torrent,
> The rapids hail the fall;
> With shouts the inland freshets
> Gather to the call.

> The quotas of the Nation,
> Like the water-shed of waves,
> Muster into union—
> Eastern warriors, Western braves.

> Martial strains are mingling,
> Though distant far the bands,
> And the wheeling of the squadrons
> Is like surf upon the sands.

> The bladed guns are gleaming—
> Drift in lengthened trim,
> Files on files for hazy miles—
> Nebulously dim.

> O Milky Way of armies—
> Star rising after star,
> New banners of the Commonwealths,
> And eagles of the War.

The Abrahamic river
To sea-wide fullness fed,
Pouring from the thaw-lands
By the God of floods is led:
> His deep enforcing current
> The streams of ocean own,
> And Europe's marge is evened
> By rills from Kansas lone.

"FORMERLY A SLAVE."

*An idealized Portrait, by E. Vedder, in the Spring
Exhibition of the National Academy, 1865.*

The sufferance of her race is shown,
  And retrospect of life,
Which now too late deliverance dawns upon;
  Yet is she not at strife.

Her children's children they shall know
  The good withheld from her;
And so her reverie takes prophetic cheer—
  In spirit she sees the stir

Far down the depth of thousand years,
  And marks the revel shine;
Her dusky face is lit with sober light,
  Sibylline, yet benign.

THE APPARITION.

(A Retrospect.)

Convulsions came; and, where the field
   Long slept in pastoral green,
A goblin-mountain was upheaved
(Sure the scared sense was all deceived),
   Marl-glen and slag-ravine.

The unreserve of Ill was there,
   The clinkers in her last retreat;
But, ere the eye could take it in,
Or mind could comprehension win,
   It sunk!—and at our feet.

So, then, Solidity's a crust—
   The core of fire below;
All may go well for many a year,
But who can think without a fear
   Of horrors that happen so?

ON THE SLAIN COLLEGIANS.

Youth is the time when hearts are large,
  And stirring wars
Appeal to the spirit which appeals in turn
  To the blade it draws.
If woman incite, and duty show
 (Though made the mask of Cain),
Or whether it be Truth's sacred cause,
  Who can aloof remain
That shares youth's ardor, uncooled by the snow
  Of wisdom or sordid gain?

The liberal arts and nurture sweet
Which give his gentleness to man—
 Train him to honor, lend him grace
Through bright examples meet—
That culture which makes never wan
With underminings deep, but holds
 The surface still, its fitting place,
 And so gives sunniness to the face
And bravery to the heart; what troops
 Of generous boys in happiness thus bred—
 Saturnians through life's Tempe led,
Went from the North and came from the South,
With golden mottoes in the mouth,
 To lie down midway on a bloody bed.

Woe for the homes of the North,
And woe for the seats of the South:
All who felt life's spring in prime,
And were swept by the wind of their place and time—
 All lavish hearts, on whichever side,
Of birth urbane or courage high,
Armed them for the stirring wars—
Armed them—some to die.
  Apollo-like in pride,
Each would slay his Python—caught
The maxims in his temple taught—

Aflame with sympathies whose blaze
Perforce enwrapped him—social laws,
  Friendship and kin, and by-gone days—
Vows, kisses—every heart unmoors,
And launches into the seas of wars.
What could they else—North or South?
Each went forth with blessings given
By priests and mothers in the name of Heaven;
    And honor in both was chief.
Warred one for Right, and one for Wrong?
So be it; but they both were young—
Each grape to his cluster clung,
All their elegies are sung.

The anguish of maternal hearts
  Must search for balm divine;
But well the striplings bore their fated parts
  (The heavens all parts assign)—
Never felt life's care or cloy.
Each bloomed and died an unabated Boy;
Nor dreamed what death was—thought it mere
Sliding into some vernal sphere.
They knew the joy, but leaped the grief,
Like plants that flower ere comes the leaf—
Which storms lay low in kindly doom,
And kill them in their flush of bloom.

AMERICA.

I.

Where the wings of a sunny Dome expand
I saw a Banner in gladsome air—
Starry, like Berenice's Hair—
Afloat in broadened bravery there;
With undulating long-drawn flow,
As rolled Brazilian billows go
Voluminously o'er the Line.
The Land reposed in peace below;
　　The children in their glee
Were folded to the exulting heart
　　Of young Maternity.

II.

Later, and it streamed in fight
　　When tempest mingled with the fray,
And over the spear-point of the shaft
　　I saw the ambiguous lightning play.
Valor with Valor strove, and died:
Fierce was Despair, and cruel was Pride;
And the lorn Mother speechless stood,
Pale at the fury of her brood.

III.

Yet later, and the silk did wind
　　　　Her fair cold form;
Little availed the shining shroud,
　　Though ruddy in hue, to cheer or warm.
A watcher looked upon her low, and said—
She sleeps, but sleeps, she is not dead.
　　But in that sleep contortion showed
The terror of the vision there—
　　A silent vision unavowed,

Revealing earth's foundation bare,
  And Gorgon in her hidden place.
It was a thing of fear to see
  So foul a dream upon so fair a face,
And the dreamer lying in that starry shroud.

IV.

But from the trance she sudden broke—
  The trance, or death into promoted life;
At her feet a shivered yoke,
And in her aspect turned to heaven
  No trace of passion or of strife—
A clear calm look. It spake of pain,
But such as purifies from stain—
Sharp pangs that never come again—
  And triumph repressed by knowledge meet,
Power dedicate, and hope grown wise,
  And youth matured for age's seat—
Law on her brow and empire in her eyes.
  So she, with graver air and lifted flag;
While the shadow, chased by light,
Fled along the far-drawn height,
  And left her on the crag.

ON THE HOME GUARDS

who perished in the Defense of Lexington, Missouri.

The men who here in harness died
    Fell not in vain, though in defeat.
They by their end well fortified
    The Cause, and built retreat
(With memory of their valor tried)
For emulous hearts in many an after fray—
Hearts sore beset, which died at bay.

THE FORTITUDE OF THE NORTH

under the Disaster of the Second Manassas.

They take no shame for dark defeat
    While prizing yet each victory won,
Who fight for the Right through all retreat,
    Nor pause until their work is done.
The Cape-of-Storms is proof to every throe;
    Vainly against that foreland beat
Wild winds aloft and wilder waves below:
    The black cliffs gleam through rents in sleet
When the livid Antarctic storm-clouds glow.

INSCRIPTION

for Marye's Heights, Fredericksburg.

To them who crossed the flood
And climbed the hill, with eyes
    Upon the heavenly flag intent,
    And through the deathful tumult went
Even unto death: to them this Stone—
Erect, where they were overthrown—
    Of more than victory the monument.

ON SHERMAN'S MEN

who fell in the Assault of Kenesaw Mountain, Georgia.

They said that Fame her clarion dropped
    Because great deeds were done no more—
That even Duty knew no shining ends,
And Glory—'twas a fallen star!
    But battle can heroes and bards restore.
        Nay, look at Kenesaw:
Perils the mailed ones never knew
Are lightly braved by the ragged coats of blue,
And gentler hearts are bared to deadlier war.

ON THE GRAVE

*of a young Cavalry Officer killed in the Valley of
Virginia.*

Beauty and youth, with manners sweet, and friends—
  Gold, yet a mind not unenriched had he
Whom here low violets veil from eyes.
  But all these gifts transcended be:
His happier fortune in this mound you see.

COMMEMORATIVE OF A NAVAL VICTORY.

Sailors there are of gentlest breed,
    Yet strong, like every goodly thing;
The discipline of arms refines,
    And the wave gives tempering.
    The damasked blade its beam can fling;
It lends the last grave grace:
The hawk, the hound, and sworded nobleman
    In Titian's picture for a king,
Are of hunter or warrior race.

In social halls a favored guest
    In years that follow victory won,
How sweet to feel your festal fame
    In woman's glance instinctive thrown:
    Repose is yours—your deed is known,
It musks the amber wine;
It lives, and sheds a light from storied days
    Rich as October sunsets brown,
Which make the barren place to shine.

But seldom the laurel wreath is seen
    Unmixed with pensive pansies dark;
There's a light and a shadow on every man
    Who at last attains his lifted mark—
    Nursing through night the ethereal spark.
Elate he never can be;
He feels that spirits which glad had hailed his worth,
    Sleep in oblivion.—The shark
Glides white through the phosphorus sea.

A *Pilgrimage:* from CLAREL

PART I, CANTO XIII

THE ARCH.

Blue-lights sent up by ship forlorn
Are answered oft but by the glare
Of rockets from another, torn
In the same gale's inclusive snare.

'Twas then when Celio was lanced
By novel doubt, the encounter chanced
In Gihon, as recited late,
And at a time when Clarel too,
On his part, felt the grievous weight
10   Of those demoniacs in view;
So that when Celio advanced
No wonder that the meeting eyes
Betrayed reciprocal surmise
And interest. 'Twas thereupon
The Italian, as the eve drew on,
Regained the gate, and hurried in
As he would passionately win
Surcease to thought by rapid pace.
Eastward he bent, across the town,
20   Till in the Via Crucis lone
An object there arrested him.
With gallery which years deface,
Its bulk athwart the alley grim,
The arch named Ecce Homo threw;
The same, if child-like faith be true,
From which the Lamb of God was shown
By Pilate to the wolfish crew.
And Celio—in frame how prone
To kindle at that scene recalled—
30   Perturbed he stood, and heart-enthralled.
No raptures which with saints prevail,
Nor trouble of compunction born
He felt, as there he seemed to scan

Aloft in spectral guise, the pale
Still face, the purple robe, and thorn;
And inly cried—*Behold the Man!*
Yon Man it is this burden lays:
Even he who in the pastoral hours,
Abroad in fields, and cheered by flowers,
Announced a heaven's unclouded days;
And, ah, with such persuasive lips—
Those lips now sealed while doom delays—
Won men to look for solace there;
But, crying out in death's eclipse,
When rainbow none his eyes might see,
Enlarged the margin for despair—
My God, my God, forsakest me?
          Upbraider! we upbraid again;
Thee we upbraid; our pangs constrain
Pathos itself to cruelty.
Ere yet thy day no pledge was given
Of homes and mansions in the heaven—
Paternal homes reserved for us;
Heart hoped it not, but lived content—
Content with life's own discontent,
Nor deemed that fate ere swerved for us:
The natural law men let prevail;
Then reason disallowed the state
Of instinct's variance with fate.
But thou—ah, see, in rack how pale
Who did the world with throes convulse;
Behold him—yea—behold the Man
Who warranted if not began
The dream that drags out its repulse.
          Nor less some cannot break from thee;
Thy love so locked is with thy lore,
They may not rend them and go free:
The head rejects; so much the more
The heart embraces—what? the love?
If true what priests avouch of thee,
The shark thou mad'st, yet claim'st the dove.
          Nature and thee in vain we search:
Well urged the Jews within the porch—

40

50

60

70

"How long wilt make us still to doubt?"
How long?—'Tis eighteen cycles now—
Enigma and evasion grow;
And shall we never find thee out?
What isolation lones thy state
That all we else know cannot mate
80   With what thou teachest? Nearing thee
All footing fails us; history
Shows there a gulf where bridge is none!
In lapse of unrecorded time,
Just after the apostles' prime,
What chance or craft might break it down?
Served this a purpose? By what art
Of conjuration might the heart
Of heavenly love, so sweet, so good,
Corrupt into the creeds malign,
90   Begetting strife's pernicious brood,
Which claimed for patron thee divine?
　　　Anew, anew,
For this thou bleedest, Anguished Face;
Yea, thou through ages to accrue,
Shalt the Medusa shield replace:
In beauty and in terror too
Shalt paralyze the nobler race—
Smite or suspend, perplex, deter—
Tortured, shalt prove a torturer.
100   Whatever ribald Future be,
Thee shall these heed, amaze their hearts with thee—
Thy white, thy red, thy fairness and thy tragedy.

　　　He turned, uptorn in inmost frame,
Nor weened he went the way he came,
Till meeting two there, nor in calm—
A monk and layman, one in creed,
The last with novice-ardor warm,
New-comer, and devout indeed,
To whom the other was the guide,
110   And showed the Places. "Here," he cried,
At pause before a wayside stone,
"Thou mark'st the spot where that bad Jew

His churlish taunt at Jesus threw
Bowed under cross with stifled moan:
Caitiff, which for that cruel wrong
Thenceforth till Doomsday drives along."
    Starting, as here he made review,
Celio winced—Am *I* the Jew?
Without delay, afresh he turns
120   Descending by the Way of Thorns,
Winning the Proto-Martyr's gate,
And goes out down Jehoshaphat.
Beside him slid the shadows flung
By evening from the tomb-stones tall
Upon the bank far sloping from the wall.
Scarce did he heed, or did but slight
The admonishment the warder rung
That with the setting of the sun,
Now getting low and all but run,
130   The gate would close, and for the night.

PART I, CANTO XXXVII

A SKETCH.

Not knowing them in very heart,
Nor why to join him they were loth,
He, disappointed, moved apart,
With sad pace creeping, dull, as doth
Along the bough the nerveless sloth.

    For ease upon the ground they sit;
And Rolfe, with eye still following
Where Nehemiah slow footed it,
Asked Clarel: "Know you anything
Of this man's prior life at all?"
"Nothing," said Clarel.—"I recall,"
Said Rolfe, "a mariner like him."
"A mariner?"—"Yes; one whom grim
Disaster made as meek as he
There plodding." Vine here showed the zest
Of a deep human interest:
"We crave of you his history:"
    And Rolfe began: "Scarce would I tell
Of what this mariner befell—
So much is it with cloud o'ercast—
Were he not now gone home at last
Into the green land of the dead,
Where he encamps and peace is shed.
Hardy he was, sanguine and bold,
The master of a ship. His mind
In night-watch frequent he unrolled—
As seamen sometimes are inclined—
On serious topics, to his mate,
A man to creed austere resigned.
The master ever spurned at fate,
Calvin's or Zeno's. Always still
Man-like he stood by man's free will
And power to effect each thing he would,
Did reason but pronounce it good.

The subaltern held in humble way
That still heaven's over-rulings sway
Will and event.
                    "On waters far,
Where map-man never made survey,
40   Gliding along in easy plight,
The strong one brake the lull of night
Emphatic in his willful war—
But staggered, for there came a jar
With fell arrest to keel and speech:
A hidden rock. The pound—the grind—
Collapsing sails o'er deck declined—
Sleek billows curling in the breach,
And nature with her neutral mind.
A wreck. 'Twas in the former days,
50   Those waters then obscure; a maze;
The isles were dreaded—every chain;
Better to brave the immense of sea,
And venture for the Spanish Main,
Beating and rowing against the trades,
Than float to valleys 'neath the lee,
Nor far removed, and palmy shades.
So deemed he, strongly erring there.
To boats they take; the weather fair—
Never the sky a cloudlet knew;
60   A temperate wind unvarying blew
Week after week; yet came despair;
The bread though doled, and water stored,
Ran low and lower—ceased. They burn—
They agonize till crime abhorred
Lawful might be. O trade-wind, turn!
        "Well may some items sleep unrolled—
Never by the one survivor told.
Him they picked up, where, cuddled down,
They saw the jacketed skeleton,
70   Lone in the only boat that lived—
His signal frittered to a shred.
        "'Strong need'st thou be,' the rescuers said,
'Who hast such trial sole survived.'
'I *willed* it,' gasped he. And the man,

Renewed ashore, pushed off again.
How bravely sailed the pennoned ship
Bound outward on her sealing trip
Antarctic. Yes; but who returns
Too soon, regaining port by land
Who left it by the bay? What spurns
Were his that so could countermand?
Nor mutineer, nor rock, nor gale
Nor leak had foiled him. No; a whale
Of purpose aiming, stove the bow:
They foundered. To the master now
Owners and neighbors all impute
An inauspiciousness. His wife—
Gentle, but unheroic—she,
Poor thing, at heart knew bitter strife
Between her love and her simplicity:
A Jonah is he?—And men bruit
The story. None will give him place
In a third venture. Came the day
Dire need constrained the man to pace
A night patrolman on the quay
Watching the bales till morning hour
Through fair and foul. Never he smiled;
Call him, and he would come; not sour
In spirit, but meek and reconciled;
Patient he was, he none withstood;
Oft on some secret thing would brood.
He ate what came, though but a crust;
In Calvin's creed he put his trust;
Praised heaven, and said that God was good,
And his calamity but just.
So Sylvio Pellico from cell-door
Forth tottering, after dungeoned years,
Crippled and bleached, and dead his peers:
'Grateful, I thank the Emperor.'"

There ceasing, after pause Rolfe drew
Regard to Nehemiah in view:
"Look, the changed master, roams he there?
I mean, is such the guise, the air?"

The speaker sat between mute Vine
And Clarel. From the mystic sea
Laocoon's serpent, sleek and fine,
In loop on loop seemed here to twine
His clammy coils about the three.
Then unto them the wannish man
120   Draws nigh; but absently they scan;
A phantom seems he, and from zone
Where naught is real though the winds aye moan.

PART II, CANTO XXVII

VINE AND CLAREL.

While now, to serve the pilgrim train,
The Arabs willow branches hew
(For palms they serve in dearth of true),
Or, kneeling by the margin, stoop
To brim memorial bottles up;
And the Greek's wine entices two:
Apart see Clarel here incline,
Perplexed by that Dominican,
Nor less by Rolfe—capricious man:
10   "I cannot penetrate him.—Vine?"
As were Venetian slats between,
He espied him through a leafy screen,
Luxurious there in umbrage thrown,
Light sprays above his temples blown—
The river through the green retreat
Hurrying, reveling by his feet.
Vine looked an overture, but said
Nothing, till Clarel leaned—half laid—
Beside him: then[,] "We dream, or be
20   In sylvan John's baptistery:
May Pisa's equal beauty keep?—
But how bad habits persevere!
I have been moralizing here
Like any imbecile: as thus:
Look how these willows over-weep
The waves, and plain: 'Fleet so from us?
And wherefore? whitherward away?
Your best is here where wildings sway
And the light shadow's blown about;
30   Ah, tarry, for at hand's a sea
Whence ye shall never issue out
Once in.' They sing back: 'So let be!
We mad-caps hymn it as we flow—

Short life and merry! be it so!'"
Surprised at such a fluent turn,
The student did but listen—learn.

Putting aside the twigs which screened,
Again Vine spake, and lightly leaned[:]
"Look; in yon vault so leafy dark,
At deep end lit by gemmy spark
Of mellowed sunbeam in a snare;
Over the stream—ay, just through there—
The sheik on that celestial mare
Shot, fading.—Clan of outcast Hagar,
Well do ye come by spear and dagger!
Yet in your bearing ye outvie
Our western Red Men, chiefs that stalk
In mud paint—whirl the tomahawk.—
But in these Nimrods noted you
The natural language of the eye,
Burning or liquid, flame or dew,
As still the changeable quick mood
Made transit in the wayward blood?
Methought therein one might espy,
For all the wildness, thoughts refined
By the old Asia's dreamful mind;
But hark—a bird?"
Pure as the rain
Which diamondeth with lucid grain,
The white swan in the April hours
Floating between two sunny showers
Upon the lake, while buds unroll;
So pure, so virginal in shrine
Of true unworldliness looked Vine.
Ah, clear sweet ether of the soul
(Mused Clarel), holding him in view.
Prior advances unreturned
Not here he recked of, while he yearned—
O, now but for communion true
And close; let go each alien theme;
Give me thyself!
But Vine, at will

Dwelling upon his wayward dream,
Nor as suspecting Clarel's thrill
Of personal longing, rambled still;
"Methinks they show a lingering trace
Of some quite unrecorded race
Such as the Book of Job implies.
What ages of refinings wise
80 Must have forerun what there is writ—
More ages than have followed it.
At Lydda late, as chance would have,
Some tribesmen from the south I saw,
Their tents pitched in the Gothic nave,
The ruined one. Disowning law,
Not lawless lived they; no, indeed;
Their chief—why, one of Sydney's clan,
A slayer, but chivalric man;
And chivalry, with all that breed
90 Was Arabic or Saracen
In source, they tell. But, as men stray
Further from Ararat away
Pity it were did they recede
In carriage, manners, and the rest;
But no, for ours the palm indeed
In bland amenities far West!
Come now, for pastime let's complain;
Grudged thanks, Columbus, for thy main!
Put back, as 'twere—assigned by fate
100 To fight crude Nature o'er again,
By slow degrees we re-create.
But then, alas, in Arab camps
No lack, they say, no lack of scamps."
        Divided mind knew Clarel here;
The heart's desire did interfere.
Thought he, How pleasant in another
Such sallies, or in thee, if said
After confidings that should wed
Our souls in one:—Ah, call me *brother!*—
110 So feminine his passionate mood
Which, long as hungering unfed,

All else rejected or withstood.
    Some inklings he let fall. But no:
Here over Vine there slid a change—
A shadow, such as thin may show
Gliding along the mountain-range
And deepening in the gorge below.
    Does Vine's rebukeful dusking say—
Why, on this vernal bank to-day,
Why bring oblations of thy pain
To one who hath his share? here fain
Would lap him in a chance reprieve?
Lives none can help ye; that believe.
Art thou the first soul tried by doubt?
Shalt prove the last? Go, live it out.
But for thy fonder dream of love
In man toward man—the soul's caress—
The negatives of flesh should prove
Analogies of non-cordialness
In spirit.—E'en such conceits could cling
To Clarel's dream of vain surmise
And imputation full of sting.
But, glancing up, unwarned he saw
What serious softness in those eyes
Bent on him. Shyly they withdraw.
Enslaver, wouldst thou but fool me
With bitter-sweet, sly sorcery,
Pride's pastime? or wouldst thou indeed,
Since things unspoken may impede,
Let flow thy nature but for bar?—
Nay, dizzard, sick these feelings are;
How findest place within thy heart
For such solicitudes apart
From Ruth?—Self-taxings.
              But a sign
Came here indicative from Vine,
Who with a reverent hushed air
His view directed toward the glade
Beyond, wherein a niche was made
Of leafage, and a kneeler there,
The meek one, on whom, as he prayed,

120

130

140

150

A golden shaft of mellow light,
Oblique through vernal cleft above,
And making his pale forehead bright,
Scintillant fell. By such a beam
From heaven descended erst the dove
On Christ emerging from the stream.
It faded; 'twas a transient ray;
And, quite unconscious of its sheen,
160   The suppliant rose and moved away,
Not dreaming that he had been seen.

When next they saw that innocent,
From prayer such cordial had he won
That all his aspect of content
As with the oil of gladness shone.
Less aged looked he. And his cheer
Took language in an action here:
The train now mustering in line,
Each pilgrim with a river-palm
170   In hand (except indeed the Jew),
The saint the head-stall need entwine
With wreathage of the same. When new
They issued from the wood, no charm
The ass found in such idle gear
Superfluous: with her long ear
She flapped it off, and the next thrust
Of hoof imprinted it in dust.
Meek hands (mused Vine), vainly ye twist
Fair garland for the realist.
180   The Hebrew, noting whither bent
Vine's glance, a word in passing lent:
"Ho, tell us how it comes to be
That thou who rank'st not with beginners
Regard have for yon chief of sinners."
"Yon chief of sinners?"
                              "So names he
Himself. For one I'll not express
How I do loathe such lowliness."

PART II, CANTO XXXI

THE INSCRIPTION.

While yet Rolfe's foot in stirrup stood,
Ere the light vault that wins the seat,
Derwent was heard: "What's this we meet?
A Cross? and—if one could but spell—
Inscription Sinaitic? Well,
Mortmain is nigh—*his* crazy freak;
Whose else? A closer view I'll seek;
I'll climb."
    In moving there aside
10   The rock's turned brow he had espied;
In rear this rock hung o'er the waste
And Nehemiah in sleep embraced
Below. The forepart gloomed Lot's wave
So nigh, the tide the base did lave.
Above, the sea-face smooth was worn
Through long attrition of that grit
Which on the waste of winds is borne.
And on the tablet high of it—
Traced in dull chalk, such as is found
20   Accessible in upper ground—
Big there between two scrawls, below
And over—a cross; three stars in row
Upright, two more for thwarting limb
Which drooped oblique.
              At Derwent's cry
The rest drew near; and every eye
Marked the device.—Thy passion's whim,
Wild Swede, mused Vine in silent heart.
"Looks like the *Southern Cross* to me,"
30   Said Clarel; "so 'tis down in chart."
"And so," said Rolfe, "'tis set in sky—
Though error slight of place prevail
In midmost star here chalked. At sea,

Bound for Peru, when south ye sail,
Startling that novel cluster strange
Peers up from low; then as ye range
Cape-ward still further, brightly higher
And higher the stranger doth aspire,
Till off the Horn, when at full hight
40   Ye slack your gaze as chilly grows the night.
But Derwent—see!" The priest having gained
Convenient lodge the text below,
They called: "What's that in curve contained
Above the stars? Read: we would know."
"Runs thus: *By one who wails the loss,*
This altar to the Slanting Cross."
"Ha! under that?" "Some crow's-foot scrawl."
"Decipher, quick! we're waiting all."
50   "Patience: for ere one try rehearse,
'Twere well to make it out. 'Tis verse."
"Verse, say you? Read." " 'Tis mystical:

" 'Emblazoned bleak in austral skies—
A heaven remote, whose starry swarm
Like Science lights but cannot warm—
Translated Cross, hast thou withdrawn,
Dim paling too at every dawn,
With symbols vain once counted wise,
And gods declined to heraldries?
60   Estranged, estranged: can friend prove so?
Aloft, aloof, a frigid sign:
How far removed, thou Tree divine,
Whose tender fruit did reach so low—
Love apples of New-Paradise!
About the wide Australian sea
The planted nations yet to be—
When, ages hence, they lift their eyes,
Tell, what shall they retain of thee?
But class thee with Orion's sword?
70   In constellations unadored,
Christ and the Giant equal prize?
The atheist cycles—*must* they be?
Fomentors as forefathers we?' "

"Mad, mad enough," the priest here cried,
Down slipping by the shelving brinks;
"But 'tis not Mortmain," and he sighed.
    "Not Mortmain?" Rolfe exclaimed. "Methinks,"
The priest, " 'tis hardly in his vein."
"How? fraught with feeling is the strain?
80   His heart's not ballasted with stone—
He's crank." "Well, well, e'en let us own
That Mortmain, Mortmain is the man.
We've then a pledge here at a glance
Our comrade's met with no mischance.
Soon he'll rejoin us." "There, amen!"
"But now to wake Nehemiah in den
Behind here.—But kind Clarel goes.
Strange how he naps nor trouble knows
Under the crag's impending block,
90   Nor fears its fall, nor recks of shock."

        Anon they mount; and much advance
Upon that chalked significance.
The student harks, and weighs each word,
Intent, he being newly stirred.

        But tarries Margoth? Yes, behind
He lingers. He placards his mind:
Scaling the crag he rudely scores
With the same chalk (how here abused!)
Left by the other, after used,
100   A sledge or hammer huge as Thor's;
A legend lending—this, to wit:
"I, *Science, I whose gain's thy loss,*
I slanted thee, thou Slanting Cross."
        But sun and rain, and wind, with grit
Driving, these haste to cancel it.

PART II, CANTO XXXIV

MORTMAIN REAPPEARS.

While now at poise the wings of shade
Outstretched overhang each ridge and glade,
Mortmain descends from Judah's hight
Through sally-port of minor glens:
Against the background of black dens
Blacker the figure glooms enhanced.
　　　Relieved from anxious fears, the group
In friendliness would have advanced
To greet, but shrank or fell adroop.
Like Hecla ice inveined with marl
And frozen cinders showed his face
Rigid and darkened. Shunning parle
He seated him aloof in place,
Hands clasped about the knees drawn up
As round the cask the binding hoop—
Condensed in self, or like a seer
Unconscious of each object near,
While yet, informed, the nerve may reach
Like wire under wave to furthest beach.
　　　By what brook Cherith had he been,
Watching it shrivel from the scene—
Or voice aerial had heard,
That now he murmured the wild word;
"But, hectored by the impious years,
What god invoke, for leave to unveil
That gulf whither tend these modern fears,
And deeps over which men crowd the sail?["]
　　　Up, as possessed, he rose anon,
And crying to the beach went down:
"Repent! repent in every land
Or hell's hot kingdom is at hand!
Yea, yea,
In pause of the artillery's boom,

While now the armed world holds its own,
The comet peers, the star dips down;
Flicker the lamps in Syria's tomb,
While Anti-Christ and Atheist set
On Anarch the red coronet!"

    "Mad John," sighed Rolfe, "dost there betray
40   The dire *Vox Clamans* of our day?"
    "Why heed him?" Derwent breathed: "alas!
Let him alone, and it will pass.—
What would he now?" Before the bay
Low bowed he there, with hand addressed
To scoop. "Unhappy, hadst thou best?"
Djalea it was; then calling low
Unto a Bethlehemite whose brow
Was wrinkled like the bat's shrunk hide—
"Your salt-song, Beltha: warn and chide."

50   "Would ye know what bitter drink
        They gave to Christ upon the Tree?
Sip the wave that laps the brink
        Of Siddim: taste, and God keep ye!
It drains the hills where alum's hid—
Drains the rock-salt's ancient bed;
        Hither unto basin fall
        The torrents from the steeps of gall—
Here is Hades' water-shed.
        Sinner, would ye that your soul
60   Bitter were and like the pool?
Sip the Sodom waters dead;
        But never from thy heart shall haste
        The Marah—yea, the after-taste."

    He closed.—Arrested as he stooped,
Did Mortmain his pale hand recall?
No; undeterred the wave he scooped,
And tried it—madly tried the gall.

PART II, CANTO XXXV

PRELUSIVE.

In Piranezi's rarer prints,
Interiors measurelessly strange,
Where the distrustful thought may range
Misgiving still—what mean the hints?
Stairs upon stairs which dim ascend
In series from plunged Bastiles drear—
Pit under pit; long tier on tier
Of shadowed galleries which impend
Over cloisters, cloisters without end;
10   The hight, the depth—the far, the near;
Ring-bolts to pillars in vaulted lanes,
And dragging Rhadamanthine chains;
These less of wizard influence lend
Than some allusive chambers closed.
   Those wards of hush are not disposed
In gibe of goblin fantasy—
Grimace—unclean diablery:
Thy wings, Imagination, span
Ideal truth in fable's seat:
20   The thing implied is one with man,
His penetralia of retreat—
The heart, with labyrinths replete:
In freaks of intimation see
Paul's "mystery of iniquity:"
Involved indeed, a blur of dream;
As, awed by scruple and restricted
In first design, or interdicted
By fate and warnings as might seem;
The inventor miraged all the maze,
30   Obscured it with prudential haze;
Nor less, if subject unto question,
The egg left, egg of the suggestion.
   Dwell on those etchings in the night,

Those touches bitten in the steel
By aqua-fortis, till ye feel
The Pauline text in gray of light;
Turn hither then and read aright.

For ye who green or gray retain
Childhood's illusion, or but feign;
As bride and suit[e] let pass a bier—
So pass the coming canto here.

PART III, CANTO XXXII

EMPTY STIRRUPS.

The gray of dawn. A tremor slight:
The trouble of imperfect light
Anew begins. In floating cloud
Midway suspended down the gorge,
A long mist trails white shreds of shroud
How languorous toward the Dead Sea's verge.
Riders in seat halt by the gate:
Why not set forth? For one they wait
Whose stirrups empty be—the Swede.
Still absent from the frater-hall
Since afternoon and vesper-call,
He, they imagined, had but sought
Some cave in keeping with his thought,
And reappear would with the light
Suddenly as the Gileadite
In Obadiah's way. But—no,
He cometh not when they would go.
Dismounting, they make search in vain;
Till Clarel—minding him again
Of something settled in his air—
A quietude beyond mere calm—
When seen from ledge beside the Palm
Reclined in nook of Bethel stair,
Thitherward led them in a thrill
Of nervous apprehension, till
Startled he stops, with eyes avert
And indicating hand.—
                          'Tis *he*—
So undisturbed, supine, inert—
The filmed orbs fixed upon the Tree—
Night's dews upon his eyelids be.
To test if breath remain, none tries:
On those thin lips a feather lies—
An eagle's, wafted from the skies.

The vow: and had the genius heard,
Benignant? nor had made delay,
But, more than taking him at word,
Quick wafted where the palm-boughs sway
In St. John's heaven? Some divined
That long had he been undermined
In frame; the brain a tocsin-bell
Overburdensome for citadel
Whose base was shattered. They refrain
From aught but that dumb look that fell
Identifying; feeling pain
That such a heart could beat, and will—
Aspire, yearn, suffer, baffled still,
And end. With monks which round them stood
Concerned, not discomposed in mood,
Interment they provided for—
Heaved a last sigh, nor tarried more.

Nay; one a little lingered there;
'Twas Rolfe. And as the rising sun,
Though viewless yet from Bethel stair,
More lit the mountains, he was won
To invocation, scarce to prayer:

"Holy Morning,
What blessed lore reservest thou,
Withheld from man, that evermore
Without surprise,
But, rather, with a hurtless scorning
In thy placid eyes,
Thou viewest all events alike?
Oh, tell me, do thy bright beams strike
The healing hills of Gilead now?"

And glanced toward the pale one near
In shadow of the crag's dark brow.—
Did Charity follow that poor bier?
It did; but Bigotry did steer:
Friars buried him without the walls

(Nor in a consecrated bed)
Where vulture unto vulture calls,
And only ill things find a friend:
There let the beak and claw contend,
There the hyena's cub be fed:
Heaven that disclaims, and him beweeps
In annual showers; and the tried spirit sleeps.

PART IV, CANTO XXI

UNGAR AND ROLFE.

["]Such earnestness! such wear and tear,
And man but a thin gossamer!"
So here the priest aside; then turned,
And, starting: "List! the vesper-bell?
Nay, nay—the hour is passed. But, oh,
He must have supped, Don Hannibal,
Ere now. Come, friends, and shall we go?
This hot discussion, let it stand
And cool; to-morrow we'll remand."
10   "Not yet, I pray," said Rolfe; "a word;"
And turned toward Ungar; "be adjured,
And tell us if for earth may be
In ripening arts, no guarantee
Of happy sequel."
     "Arts are tools;
But tools, they say are to the strong:
Is Satan weak? weak is the Wrong?
No blessed augury overrules:
Your arts advance in faith's decay:
20 You are but drilling the new Hun
Whose growl even now can some dismay;
Vindictive in his heart of hearts,
He schools him in your mines and marts—
A skilled destroyer."
     "But, need own
That portent does in no degree
Westward impend, across the sea."
     "Over there? And do ye not forebode?
Against pretenses void or weak
30 The impieties of 'Progress' speak.
What say *these*, in effect, to God?
'How profits it? And who art Thou
That we should serve Thee? Of Thy ways
No knowledge we desire; *new* ways
We have found out, and better. Go—

Depart from us; we do erase
Thy sinecure: behold, the sun
Stands still no more in Ajalon:
Depart from us!'—And if He do?

40   (And that He may, the Scripture says)
Is aught betwixt ye and the hells?
For He, nor in irreverent view,
'Tis He distills that savor true
Which keeps good essences from taint;
Where He is not, corruption dwells,
And man and chaos are without restraint."
    "Oh, oh, you do but generalize
In void abstractions."
                        "Hypothesize:

50   If be a people which began
Without impediment, or let
From any ruling which fore-ran;
Even striving all things to forget
But this—the excellence of man
Left to himself, his natural bent,
His own devices and intent;
And if, in satire of the heaven,
A world, a new world have been given
For stage whereon to deploy the event;

60   If such a people be——well, well,
One hears the kettle-drums of hell!
Exemplary act awaits its place
In drama of the human race."
    "Is such act certain?" Rolfe here ran;
"Not much is certain."
                        "God is—man.
The human nature, the divine—
Have both been proved by many a sign.
'Tis no astrologer and star.

70   The world has now so old become,
Historic memory goes so far
Backward through long defiles of doom;
Whoso consults it honestly
That mind grows prescient in degree;
For man, like God, abides the same

Always, through all variety
Of woven garments to the frame."
    "Yes, God is God, and men are men,
Forever and for aye. What then?
80   There's Circumstance—there's Time; and these
Are charged with store of latencies
Still working in to modify.
For mystic text that you recall,
Dilate upon, and e'en apply—
(Although I seek not to decry)
Theology's scarce practical.
But leave this: the New World's the theme,
Here, to oppose your dark extreme.
(Since an old friend is good at need)
90   To an old thought I'll fly. Pray, heed:
Those waste-weirs which the New World yields
To inland freshets—the free vents
Supplied to turbid elements;
The vast reserves—the untried fields;
These long shall keep off and delay
The class-war, rich-and-poor-man fray
Of history. From that alone
Can serious trouble spring. Even that
Itself, this good result may own—
100   The first firm founding of the state."
        Here ending, with a watchful air
Inquisitive, Rolfe waited him.
And Ungar:
            "True heart do ye bear
In this discussion? or but trim
To draw my monomania out,
For monomania, past doubt,
Some of ye deem it. Yet I'll on.
Yours seems a reasonable tone;
110   But in the New World things make haste:
Not only men, the *state* lives fast—
Fast breeds the pregnant eggs and shells,
The slumberous combustibles
Sure to explode. 'Twill come, 'twill come!
One demagogue can trouble much:

How of a hundred thousand such?
And universal suffrage lent
To back them with brute element
Overwhelming? What shall bind these seas
120   Of rival sharp communities
Unchristianized? Yea, but 'twill come!"
        "What come?"
                    "Your Thirty Years (of) War."
        "Should fortune's favorable star
Avert it?"
                    "Fortune? nay, 'tis doom."
"Then what comes after? spasms but tend
Ever, at last, to quiet."
                    "Know,
130   Whatever happen in the end,
Be sure 'twill yield to one and all
New confirmation of the fall
Of Adam. Sequel may ensue,
Indeed, whose germs one now may view:
Myriads playing pygmy parts—
Debased into equality:
In glut of all material arts
A civic barbarism may be:
Man disennobled—brutalized
140   By popular science—Atheized
Into a smatterer——"
                    "Oh, oh!"
        "Yet knowing all self need to know
In self's base little fallacy;
Dead level of rank commonplace:
An Anglo-Saxon China, see,
May on your vast plains shame the race
In the Dark Ages of Democracy."

        America!
150   In stilled estate,
On him, half-brother and co-mate—
In silence, and with vision dim
Rolfe, Vine, and Clarel gazed on him;
They gazed, nor one of them found heart

To upbraid the crotchet of his smart,
Bethinking them whence sole it came,
Though birthright he renounced in hope,
Their sanguine country's wonted claim.
Nor dull they were in honest tone
160 To some misgivings of their own:
They felt how far beyond the scope
Of elder Europe's saddest thought
Might be the New World's sudden brought
In youth to share old age's pains—
To feel the arrest of hope's advance,
And squandered last inheritance;
And cry—"To Terminus build fanes!
Columbus ended earth's romance:
No New World to mankind remains!"

PART IV, CANTO XXII

OF WICKEDNESS THE WORD.

Since, for the charity they knew,
None cared the exile to upbraid
Or further breast—while yet he threw,
In silence that oppressive weighed,
The after-influence of his spell—
The priest in light disclaimer said
To Rolfe apart: "The icicle,
The dagger-icicle draws blood;
But give it sun!" "You mean his mood
10   Is accident—would melt away
In fortune's favorable ray.
But if 'tis happiness he lacks,
Why, let the gods warm all cold backs
With that good sun. But list!"
                              In vent
Of thought, abrupt the malcontent:
"What incantation shall make less
The ever-upbubbling wickedness!
Is this fount nature's?"
20   Under guard
Asked Vine: "Is wickedness the word?"
"The right word? Yes; but scarce the *thing*
Is there conveyed; for one need know
Wicked has been the tampering
With wickedness the word." "Even so?"
"Ay, ridicule's light sacrilege
Has taken off the honest edge—
Quite turned aside—perverted all
That Saxon term and Scriptural."
30   "Restored to the incisive wedge,
What means it then, this wickedness?"
Ungar regarded him with look
Of steady search: "And wilt thou brook?

Thee leaves it whole?—This wickedness
(Might it retake true import well)
Means not default, nor vulgar vice,
Nor Adam's lapse in Paradise;
But worse: 'twas this evoked the hell—
Gave in the conscious soul's recess
40   Credence to Calvin. What's implied
In that deep utterance decried
Which Christians labially confess—
Be born anew?"

                "Ah, overstate
Thou dost!" the priest sighed; "but look there!
No jarring theme may violate
Yon tender evening sky! How fair
These olive-orchards: see, the sheep
Mild drift toward the folds of sleep.
50   The blessed Nature! still her glance
Returns the love she well receives
From hearts that with the stars advance,
Each heart that in the goal believes!"

      Ungar, though nettled, as might be,
At these bland substitutes in plea
(By him accounted so) yet sealed
His lips. In fine, all seemed to yield
With one consent a truce to talk.
But Clarel, who, since that one hour
60   Of unreserve on Saba's tower,
Less relished Derwent's pleasant walk
Of myrtles, hardly might remain
Uninfluenced by Ungar's vein:
If man in truth be what you say,
And such the prospects for the clay,
And outlook of the future—cease!
What's left us but the senses' sway?
Sinner, sin out life's petty lease:
We are not worth the saving. Nay,
70   For me, if thou speak true—but ah,
Yet, yet there gleams one beckoning star—

So near the horizon, judge I right
That 'tis of heaven?
                    But wanes the light—
The evening *Angelus* is rolled:
They rise, and seek the convent's fold.

PART IV, CANTO XXXIV

VIA CRUCIS.

Some leading thoroughfares of man
In wood-path, track, or trail began;
Though threading heart of proudest town,
They follow in controlling grade
A hint or dictate, nature's own,
By man, as by the brute, obeyed.

Within Jerusalem a lane,
Narrow, nor less an artery main
(Though little knoweth it of din),
10   In part suggests such origin.
The restoration or repair,
Successive through long ages there,
Of city upon city tumbled,
Might scarce divert that thoroughfare,
Whose hill abideth yet unhumbled
Above the valley-side it meets.
Pronounce its name, this natural street's:
The *Via Crucis*—even the way
Tradition claims to be the one
20   Trod on that Friday far away
By Him our pure exemplar shown.

'Tis Whitsun-tide. From paths without,
Through Stephen's gate—by many a vein
Convergent brought within this lane,
Ere sun-down shut the loiterer out—
As 'twere a frieze, behold the train!
Bowed water-carriers; Jews with staves,
Infirm gray monks; over-loaded slaves;
Turk soldiers—young, with home-sick eyes;
30   A Bey, bereaved through luxuries;
Strangers and exiles; Moslem dames
Long-veiled in monumental white,
Dumb from the mounds which memory claims;
A half-starved vagrant Edomite;

Sore-footed Arab girls, which toil
Depressed under heap of garden-spoil;
The patient ass with panniered urn;
Sour camels humped by heaven and man,
Whose languid necks through habit turn
For ease—for ease they hardly gain.
In varied forms of fate they wend—
Or man or animal, 'tis one:
Cross-bearers all, alike they tend
And follow, slowly follow on.

But, lagging after, who is he
Called early every hope to test,
And now, at close of rarer quest,
Finds so much more the heavier tree?
From slopes whence even Echo's gone,
Wending, he murmurs in low tone:
"They wire the world—far under sea
They talk; but never comes to me
A message from beneath the stone."

Dusked Olivet he leaves behind,
And, taking now a slender wynd,
Vanishes in the obscurer town.

PART IV, CANTO XXXV

EPILOGUE.

If Luther's day expand to Darwin's year,
Shall that exclude the hope—foreclose the fear?

Unmoved by all the claims our times avow,
The ancient Sphinx still keeps the porch of shade;
And comes Despair, whom not her calm may cow,
And coldly on that adamantine brow
Scrawls undeterred his bitter pasquinade.
But Faith (who from the scrawl indignant turns)
With blood warm oozing from her wounded trust,
10   Inscribes even on her shards of broken urns
The sign o' the cross—*the spirit above the dust!*

Yea, ape and angel, strife and old debate—
The harps of heaven and dreary gongs of hell;
Science the feud can only aggravate—
No umpire she betwixt the chimes and knell:
The running battle of the star and clod
Shall run forever—if there be no God.

Degrees we know, unknown in days before;
The light is greater, hence the shadow more;
20   And tantalized and apprehensive Man
Appealing—Wherefore ripen us to pain?
Seems there the spokesman of dumb Nature's train.
But through such strange illusions have they
passed
Who in life's pilgrimage have baffled striven—
Even death may prove unreal at the last,
And stoics be astounded into heaven.

Then keep thy heart, though yet but ill-resigned—
Clarel, thy heart, the issues there but mind;
That like the crocus budding through the snow—
30   That like a swimmer rising from the deep—
That like a burning secret which doth go
Even from the bosom that would hoard and keep;
Emerge thou mayst from the last whelming sea,
And prove that death but routs life into victory.

Sailors and the Sea

JOHN MARR.

John Marr, toward the close of the last century born in America of a mother unknown, and from boyhood up to maturity a sailor under divers flags, disabled at last from further maritime life by a crippling wound received at close quarters with pirates of the Keys, eventually betakes himself for a livelihood to less active employment ashore. There, too, he transfers his rambling disposition acquired as a sea-farer.

After a variety of removals, at first as a sail-maker from sea-port to sea-port, then adventurously inland as a rough bench-carpenter, he, finally, in the last-named capacity, settles down about the year 1838 upon what was then a frontier-prairie, sparsely sprinkled with small oak-groves and yet fewer log-houses of a little colony but recently from one of our elder inland States. Here, putting a period to his rovings, he marries.

Ere long a fever, the bane of new settlements on teeming loam, and whose sallow livery was certain to show itself, after an interval, in the complexions of too many of these people, carries off his young wife and infant child. In one coffin, put together by his own hands, they are committed with meager rites to the earth—another mound, though a small one, in the wide prairie, nor far from where the mound-builders of a race only conjecturable had left their pottery and bones, one common clay, under a strange terrace serpentine in form.

With an honest stillness in his general mien—swarthy and black-browed, with eyes that could soften or flash, but never harden, yet disclosing at times a melancholy depth—this kinless man had affections which, once placed, not readily could be dislodged or resigned to a substituted object. Being now arrived at middle-life, he resolves never to quit

the soil that holds the only beings ever connected
with him by love in the family tie. His log-house he
lets to a new-comer, one glad enough to get it, and
dwells with the household.

While the acuter sense of his bereavement be-
comes mollified by time, the void at heart abides.
Fain, if possible, would he fill that void by cultivat-
ing social relations yet nearer than before with a
people whose lot he purposes sharing to the end—
relations superadded to that mere work-a-day bond
arising from participation in the same outward hard-
ships, making reciprocal helpfulness a matter of
course. But here, and nobody to blame, he is ob-
structed.

More familiarly to consort, men of a practical
turn must sympathetically converse, and upon top-
ics of real life. But, whether as to persons or events,
one cannot always be talking about the present,
much less speculating about the future; one must
needs recur to the past, which, with the mass of
men, where the past is in any personal way a com-
mon inheritance, supplies to most practical natures
the basis of sympathetic communion.

But the past of John Marr was not the past of
these pioneers. Their hands had rested on the plow-
tail, his upon the ship's helm. They knew but their
own kind and their own usages; to him had been re-
vealed something of the checkered globe. So limited
unavoidably was the mental reach, and by conse-
quence the range of sympathy, in this particular
band of domestic emigrants, hereditary tillers of the
soil, that the ocean, but a hearsay to their fathers,
had now through yet deeper inland removal become
to themselves little more than a rumor traditional
and vague.

They were a staid people; staid through habitua-
tion to monotonous hardship; ascetics by necessity
not less than through moral bias; nearly all of them
sincerely, however narrowly, religious. They were
kindly at need, after their fashion; but to a man

wonted—as John Marr in his previous homeless so-
journings could not but have been—to the free-and-
easy tavern-clubs affording cheap recreation of an
evening in certain old and comfortable sea-port
towns of that time, and yet more familiar with the
companionship afloat of the sailors of the same pe-
riod, something was lacking. That something was
geniality, the flower of life springing from some
sense of joy in it, more or less. This their lot could
not give to these hard-working endurers of the dis-
piriting malaria,—men to whom a holiday never
came,—and they had too much of uprightness and
no art at all or desire to affect what they did not
really feel. At a corn-husking, their least grave of
gatherings, did the lone-hearted mariner seek to di-
vert his own thoughts from sadness, and in some
degree interest theirs, by adverting to aught re-
moved from the crosses and trials of their personal
surroundings, naturally enough he would slide into
some marine story or picture, but would soon recoil
upon himself and be silent, finding no encourage-
ment to proceed. Upon one such occasion an elderly
man—a blacksmith, and at Sunday gatherings an
earnest exhorter—honestly said to him, "Friend, we
know nothing of that here."

Such unresponsiveness in one's fellow-creatures
set apart from factitious life, and by their vocation
—in those days little helped by machinery—standing,
as it were, next of kin to Nature; this, to John
Marr, seemed of a piece with the apathy of Nature
herself as envisaged to him here on a prairie where
none but the perished mound-builders had as yet
left a durable mark.

The remnant of Indians thereabout—all but ex-
terminated in their recent and final war with regular
white troops, a war waged by the Red Men for their
native soil and natural rights—had been coerced
into the occupancy of wilds not very far beyond the
Mississippi—wilds *then*, but now the seats of mu-
nicipalities and States. Prior to that, the bisons,

once streaming countless in processional herds, or browsing as in an endless battle-line over these vast aboriginal pastures, had retreated, dwindled in number, before the hunters, in main a race distinct from the agricultural pioneers, though generally their advance-guard. Such a double exodus of man and beast left the plain a desert, green or blossoming indeed, but almost as forsaken as the Siberian Obi. Save the prairie-hen, sometimes startled from its lurking-place in the rank grass; and, in their migratory season, pigeons, high overhead on the wing, in dense multitudes eclipsing the day like a passing storm-cloud; save these—there being no wide woods with their underwood—birds were strangely few.

Blank stillness would for hours reign unbroken on this prairie. "It is the bed of a dried-up sea," said the companionless sailor—no geologist—to himself, musing at twilight upon the fixed undulations of that immense alluvial expanse bounded only by the horizon, and missing there the stir that, to alert eyes and ears, animates at all times the apparent solitudes of the deep.

But a scene quite at variance with one's antecedents may yet prove suggestive of them. Hooped round by a level rim, the prairie was to John Marr a reminder of ocean.

With some of his former shipmates, *chums* on certain cruises, he had contrived, prior to this last and more remote removal, to keep up a little correspondence at odd intervals. But from tidings of anybody or any sort he, in common with the other settlers, was now cut off; quite cut off, except from such news as might be conveyed over the grassy billows by the last-arrived prairie-schooner—the vernacular term, in those parts and times, for the emigrant-wagon arched high over with sail-cloth and voyaging across the vast champaign. There was no reachable post-office as yet; not even the rude little receptive box with lid and leather hinges, set up at convenient intervals on a stout stake along some solitary green way, affording a perch for birds, and which, later in the unintermitting advance of the frontier, would perhaps decay into a mossy monument, attesting yet another successive over-leaped limit of civilized life; a life which in America can to-day hardly be said to have any western bound but the ocean that washes Asia. Throughout these plains, now in places overpopulous with towns over-opulent; sweeping plains, elsewhere fenced off in every direction into flourishing farms—pale towns-men and hale farmers alike, in part, the descendants of the first sallow settlers; a region that half a cen-tury ago produced little for the sustenance of man, but to-day launching its superabundant wheat-har-vest on the world;—of this prairie, now everywhere intersected with wire and rail, hardly can it be said that at the period here written of there was so much as a traceable road. To the long-distance traveler the oak-groves, wide apart, and varying in compass and form; these, with recent settlements, yet more widely separate, offered some landmarks; but other-wise he steered by the sun. In early midsummer, even going but from one log-encampment to the next, a journey it might be of hours or good part of a day, travel was much like navigation. In some more enriched depressions between the long, green, graduated swells, smooth as those of ocean be-calmed receiving and subduing to its own tranquil-lity the voluminous surge raised by some far-off hurricane of days previous, here one would catch the first indication of advancing strangers either in the distance, as a far sail at sea, by the glistening white canvas of the wagon, the wagon itself wading through the rank vegetation and hidden by it, or, failing that, when near to, in the ears of the team, peaking, if not above the tall tiger-lilies, yet above the yet taller grass.

Luxuriant, this wilderness; but, to its denizen, a friend left behind anywhere in the world seemed not alone absent to sight, but an absentee from existence.

Though John Marr's shipmates could not all have departed life, yet as subjects of meditation they were like phantoms of the dead. As the growing sense of his environment threw him more and more upon retrospective musings, these phantoms, next to those of his wife and child, became spiritual companions, losing something of their first indistinctness and putting on at last a dim semblance of mute life; and they were lit by that aureola circling over any object of the affections in the past for reunion with which an imaginative heart passionately yearns.

He invokes these visionary ones,—striving, as it were, to get into verbal communion with them, or, under yet stronger illusion, reproaching them for their silence:—

Since as in night's deck-watch ye show,
Why, lads, so silent here to me,
Your watchmate of times long ago?

Once, for all the darkling sea,
You your voices raised how clearly,
Striking in when tempest sung;
Hoisting up the storm-sail cheerly,
Life is storm—let storm! you rung.
Taking things as fated merely,
Child-like though the world ye spanned;
Nor holding unto life too dearly,
Ye who held your lives in hand—
Skimmers, who on oceans four
Petrels were, and larks ashore.

O, not from memory lightly flung,
Forgot, like strains no more availing,
The heart to music haughtier strung;
Nay, frequent near me, never staleing,

Whose .good feeling kept ye young.
Like tides that enter creek or stream,
Ye come, ye visit me, or seem
Swimming out from seas of faces,
Alien myriads memory traces,
To enfold me in a dream!

I yearn as ye. But rafts that strain,
Parted, shall they lock again?
Twined we were, entwined, then riven,
Ever to new embracements driven,
Shifting gulf-weed of the main!
And how if one here shift no more,
Lodged by the flinging surge ashore?

Nor less, as now, in eve's decline,
Your shadowy fellowship is mine.
Ye float around me, form and feature:—
Tattooings, ear-rings, love-locks curled;
Barbarians of man's simpler nature,
Unworldly servers of the world.
Yea, present all, and dear to me,
Though shades, or scouring China's sea.

Whither, whither, merchant-sailors,
Whitherward now in roaring gales?
Competing still, ye huntsman-whalers,
In leviathan's wake what boat prevails?
And man-of-war's men, whereaway?
If now no dinned drum beat to quarters
On the wilds of midnight waters—
Foemen looming through the spray;
Do yet your gangway lanterns, streaming,
Vainly strive to pierce below,
When, tilted from the slant plank gleaming,
A brother you see to darkness go?

But, gunmates lashed in shotted canvas,
If where long watch-below ye keep,
Never the shrill "*All hands up hammocks!*"
Breaks the spell that charms your sleep,

And summoning trumps might vainly call,
And booming guns implore—
A beat, a heart-beat musters all,
One heart-beat at heart-core.
It musters. But to clasp, retain;
To see you at the halyards main—
To hear your chorus once again!

TOM DEADLIGHT.

(1810.)

During a tempest encountered homeward-bound
from the Mediterranean, a grizzled petty-officer, one
of the two captains of the forecastle, dying at night
in his hammock, swung in the *sick-bay* under the
tiered gun-decks of the British *Dreadnaught*, 98,
wandering in his mind, though with glimpses of
sanity, and starting up at whiles, sings by snatches
his good-bye and last injunctions to two messmates,
his watchers, one of whom fans the fevered tar with
the flap of his old sou'-wester. Some names and
phrases, with here and there a line, or part of one;
these, in his aberration, wrested into incoherency
from their original connection and import, he invol-
untarily derives, as he does the measure, from a fa-
mous old sea-ditty, whose cadences, long rife, and
now humming in the collapsing brain, attune the
last flutterings of distempered thought.

Farewell and adieu to you noble hearties,—
    Farewell and adieu to you ladies of Spain,
For I've received orders for to sail for the Deadman,
    But hope with the grand fleet to see you again.

I have hove my ship to, with main-top-sail aback,
        boys;
    I have hove my ship to, for to strike soundings
        clear—
The black scud a' flying; but, by God's blessing, dam'
        me,
    Right up the Channel for the Deadman I'll steer.

I have worried through the waters that are callèd the
    Doldrums,
    And growled at Sargasso that clogs while ye grope—
Blast my eyes, but the light-ship is hid by the mist,
    lads:—
    Flying Dutchman—odds bobbs—off the Cape of
    Good Hope!

But what's this I feel that is fanning my cheek, Matt?
    The white goney's wing?—how she rolls!—'t is the
    Cape!—
Give my kit to the mess, Jock, for kin none is mine,
    none;
    And tell *Holy Joe* to avast with the crape.

Dead reckoning, says *Joe*, it won't do to go by;
    But they doused all the glims, Matt, in sky t' other
    night.
Dead reckoning is good for to sail for the Deadman;
    And Tom Deadlight he thinks it may reckon near
    right.

The signal!—it streams for the grand fleet to anchor.
    The captains—the trumpets—the hullabaloo!
Stand by for blue-blazes, and mind your shank-
    painters,
    For the Lord High Admiral, he's squinting at you!

But give me my *tot*, Matt, before I roll over;
    Jock, let's have your flipper, it's good for to feel;
And don't sew me up without *baccy* in mouth, boys,
    And don't blubber like lubbers when I turn up my
    keel.

JACK ROY.

Kept up by relays of generations young
Never dies at halyards the blithe chorus sung;
While in sands, sounds, and seas where the storm-petrels cry,
Dropped mute around the globe, these halyard singers lie.
Short-lived the clippers for racing-cups that run,
And speeds in life's career many a lavish mother's-son.

But thou, manly king o' the old *Splendid's* crew,
The ribbons o' thy hat still a-fluttering, should fly—
A challenge, and forever, nor the bravery should rue.
Only in a tussle for the starry flag high,
When 't is piety to do, and privilege to die,

Then, only then, would heaven think to lop
Such a cedar as the captain o' the *Splendid's* main-top:
A belted sea-gentleman; a gallant, off-hand
Mercutio indifferent in life's gay command.
Magnanimous in humor; when the splintering shot fell,
"Tooth-picks a-plenty, lads; thank 'em with a shell!"

Sang Larry o' the Cannakin, smuggler o' the wine,
At mess between guns, lad in jovial recline:
"In Limbo our Jack he would chirrup up a cheer,
The martinet there find a chaffing mutineer;
From a thousand fathoms down under hatches o' your Hades,
He'd ascend in love-ditty, kissing fingers to your ladies!"

Never relishing the knave, though allowing for the menial,
Nor overmuch the king, Jack, nor prodigally genial.
Ashore on liberty, he flashed in escapade,
Vaulting over life in its levelness of grade,
Like the dolphin off Africa in rainbow a-sweeping—
Arch iridescent shot from seas languid sleeping.

Larking with thy life, if a joy but a toy,
Heroic in thy levity wert thou, Jack Roy.

THE HAGLETS.

By chapel bare, with walls sea-beat,
The lichened urns in wilds are lost
About a carved memorial stone
That shows, decayed and coral-mossed,
A form recumbent, swords at feet,
Trophies at head, and kelp for a winding-sheet.

I invoke thy ghost, neglected fane,
Washed by the waters' long lament;
I adjure the recumbent effigy
To tell the cenotaph's intent—
Reveal why fagotted swords are at feet,
Why trophies appear and weeds are the winding-sheet.

By open ports the Admiral sits,
And shares repose with guns that tell
Of power that smote the arm'd Plate Fleet
Whose sinking flag-ship's colors fell;
But over the Admiral floats in light
His squadron's flag, the red-cross Flag of the White.
    The eddying waters whirl astern,
The prow, a seedsman, sows the spray;
With bellying sails and buckling spars
The black hull leaves a Milky Way;
Her timbers thrill, her batteries roll,
She revelling speeds exulting with pennon at pole.
    But ah, for standards captive trailed
For all their scutcheoned castles' pride—
Castilian towers that dominate Spain,
Naples, and either Ind beside;
Those haughty towers, armorial ones,
Rue the salute from the Admiral's dens of guns.

Ensigns and arms in trophy brave,
Braver for many a rent and scar,
The captor's naval hall bedeck,
Spoil that insures an earldom's star—
Toledoes great, grand draperies too,
Spain's steel and silk, and splendors from Peru.
  But crippled part in splintering fight,
The vanquished flying the victor's flags,
With prize-crews, under convoy-guns,
Heavy the fleet from Opher drags—
The Admiral crowding sail ahead,
Foremost with news who foremost in conflict sped.
  But out from cloistral gallery dim,
In early night his glance is thrown;
He marks the vague reserve of heaven,
He feels the touch of ocean lone;
Then turns, in frame part undermined,
Nor notes the shadowing wings that fan behind.

There, peaked and gray, three haglets fly,
And follow, follow fast in wake
Where slides the cabin-lustre shy,
And sharks from man a glamour take,
Seething along the line of light
In lane that endless rules the war-ship's flight.
  The sea-fowl here, whose hearts none know,
They followed late the flag-ship quelled,
(As now the victor one) and long
Above her gurgling grave, shrill held
With screams their wheeling rites—then sped
Direct in silence where the victor led.
  Now winds less fleet, but fairer, blow,
A ripple laps the coppered side,
While phosphor sparks make ocean gleam,
Like camps lit up in triumph wide;
With lights and tinkling cymbals meet
Acclaiming seas the advancing conqueror greet.

But who a flattering tide may trust,
Or favoring breeze, or aught in end?—
Careening under startling blasts

The sheeted towers of sails impend;
While, gathering bale, behind is bred
A livid storm-bow, like a rainbow dead.
  At trumpet-call the topmen spring;
And, urged by after-call in stress,
Yet other tribes of tars ascend
The rigging's howling wilderness;
But ere yard-ends alert they win,
Hell rules in heaven with hurricane-fire and din.
  The spars, athwart at spiry height,
Like quaking Lima's crosses rock;
Like bees the clustering sailors cling
Against the shrouds, or take the shock
Flat on the swept yard-arms aslant,
Dipped like the wheeling condor's pinions gaunt.

A lull! and tongues of languid flame
Lick every boom, and lambent show
Electric 'gainst each face aloft;
The herds of clouds with bellowings go:
The black ship rears—beset—harassed,
Then plunges far with luminous antlers vast.
  In trim betimes they turn from land,
Some shivered sails and spars they stow;
One watch, dismissed, they troll the can,
While loud the billow thumps the bow—
Vies with the fist that smites the board,
Obstreperous at each reveller's jovial word.
  Of royal oak by storms confirmed,
The tested hull her lineage shows:
Vainly the plungings whelm her prow—
She rallies, rears, she sturdier grows;
Each shot-hole plugged, each storm-sail home,
With batteries housed she rams the watery dome.

Dim seen adrift through driving scud,
The wan moon shows in plight forlorn;
Then, pinched in visage, fades and fades
Like to the faces drowned at morn,
When deeps engulfed the flag-ship's crew,
And, shrilling round, the inscrutable haglets flew.

And still they fly, nor now they cry,
But constant fan a second wake,
Unflagging pinions ply and ply,
Abreast their course intent they take;
Their silence marks a stable mood,
They patient keep their eager neighborhood.
    Plumed with a smoke, a confluent sea,
Heaved in a combing pyramid full,
Spent at its climax, in collapse
Down headlong thundering stuns the hull:
The trophy drops; but, reared again,
Shows Mars' high-altar and contemns the main.

Rebuilt it stands, the brag of arms,
Transferred in site—no thought of where
The sensitive needle keeps its place,
And starts, disturbed, a quiverer there;
The helmsman rubs the clouded glass—
Peers in, but lets the trembling portent pass.
    Let pass as well his shipmates do
(Whose dream of power no tremors jar)
Fears for the fleet convoyed astern:
"Our flag they fly, they share our star;
Spain's galleons great in hull are stout:
Manned by our men—like us they'll ride it out."
    To-night's the night that ends the week—
Ends day and week and month and year:
A fourfold imminent flickering time,
For now the midnight draws anear:
Eight bells! and passing-bells they be—
The Old Year fades, the Old Year dies at sea.

He launched them well. But shall the New
Redeem the pledge the Old Year made,
Or prove a self-asserting heir?
But healthy hearts few qualms invade:
By shot-chests grouped in bays 'tween guns
The gossips chat, the grizzled, sea-beat ones.
    And boyish dreams some graybeards blab:
"To sea, my lads, we go no more
Who share the Acapulco prize;

We'll all night in, and bang the door;
Our ingots red shall yield us bliss:
Lads, golden years begin to-night with this!"
    Released from deck, yet waiting call,
Glazed caps and coats baptized in storm,
A watch of Laced Sleeves round the board
Draw near in heart to keep them warm:
"Sweethearts and wives!" clink, clink, they meet,
And, quaffing, dip in wine their beards of sleet.

"Ay, let the star-light stay withdrawn,
So here her hearth-light memory fling,
So in this wine-light cheer be born,
And honor's fellowship weld our ring—
Honor! our Admiral's aim foretold:
A *tomb or a trophy*, and lo, 'tis a trophy and gold!"
    But he, a unit, sole in rank,
Apart needs keep his lonely state,
The sentry at his guarded door
Mute as by vault the sculptured Fate;
Belted he sits in drowsy light,
And, hatted, nods—the Admiral of the White.
    He dozes, aged with watches passed—
Years, years of pacing to and fro;
He dozes, nor attends the stir
In bullioned standards rustling low,
Nor minds the blades whose secret thrill
Perverts overhead the magnet's Polar will;—

Less heeds the shadowing three that ply
And follow, follow fast in wake,
Untiring wing and lidless eye—
Abreast their course intent they take;
Or sigh or sing, they hold for good
The unvarying flight and fixed inveterate mood.
    In dream at last his dozings merge,
In dream he reaps his victory's fruit:
The Flags-o'-the-Blue, the Flags-o'-the-Red,
Dipped flags of his country's fleets salute
His Flag-o'-the-White in harbor proud—
But why should it blench? Why turn to a painted shroud?

The hungry seas they hound the hull,
The sharks they dog the haglets' flight;
With one consent the winds, the waves
In hunt with fins and wings unite,
While drear the harps in cordage sound
Remindful wails for old Armadas drowned.

Ha—yonder! are they Northern Lights?
Or signals flashed to warn or ward?
Yea, signals lanced in breakers high;
But doom on warning follows hard:
While yet they veer in hope to shun,
They strike! and thumps of hull and heart are one.

But beating hearts a drum-beat calls
And prompt the men to quarters go;
Discipline, curbing nature, rules—
Heroic makes who duty know:
They execute the trump's command,
Or in peremptory places wait and stand.

Yet cast about in blind amaze—
As through their watery shroud they peer:
"We tacked from land: then how betrayed?
Have currents swerved us—snared us here?"
None heed the blades that clash in place
Under lamps dashed down that lit the magnet's case.

Ah, what may live, who mighty swim,
Or boat-crew reach that shore forbid,
Or cable span? Must victors drown—
Perish, even as the vanquished did?
Man keeps from man the stifled moan;
They shouldering stand, yet each in heart how lone.

Some heaven invoke; but rings of reefs
Prayer and despair alike deride
In dance of breakers forked or peaked,
Pale maniacs of the maddened tide;
While, strenuous yet some end to earn,
The haglets spin, though now no more astern.

Like shuttles hurrying in the looms
Aloft through rigging frayed they ply—
Cross and recross—weave and inweave,

Then lock the web with clinching cry
Over the seas on seas that clasp
The weltering wreck where gurgling ends the gasp.

Ah, for the Plate-Fleet trophy now,
The victor's voucher, flags and arms;
Never they'll hang in Abbey old
And take Time's dust with holier palms;
Nor less content, in liquid night,
Their captor sleeps—the Admiral of the White.

Imbedded deep with shells
And drifted treasure deep,
Forever he sinks deeper in
Unfathomable sleep—
His cannon round him thrown,
His sailors at his feet,
The wizard sea enchanting them
Where never haglets beat.

On nights when meteors play
And light the breakers' dance,
The Oreads from the caves
With silvery elves advance;
And up from ocean stream,
And down from heaven far,
The rays that blend in dream
The abysm and the star.

THE ÆOLIAN HARP

At the Surf Inn.

List the harp in window wailing
   Stirred by fitful gales from sea:
Shrieking up in mad crescendo—
   Dying down in plaintive key!

Listen: less a strain ideal
   Than Ariel's rendering of the Real.
What that Real is, let hint
   A picture stamped in memory's mint.

Braced well up, with beams aslant,
Betwixt the continents sails the *Phocion*,
For Baltimore bound from Alicant.
Blue breezy skies white fleeces fleck
Over the chill blue white-capped ocean:
From yard-arm comes—"Wreck ho, a wreck!"

Dismasted and adrift,
Long time a thing forsaken;
Overwashed by every wave
Like the slumbering kraken;
Heedless if the billow roar,
Oblivious of the lull,
Leagues and leagues from shoal or shore,
It swims—a levelled hull:
Bulwarks gone—a shaven wreck,
Nameless, and a grass-green deck.
A lumberman: perchance, in hold
Prostrate pines with hemlocks rolled.

It has drifted, waterlogged,
Till by trailing weeds beclogged:
   Drifted, drifted, day by day,
   Pilotless on pathless way.
It has drifted till each plank

Is oozy as the oyster-bank:
  Drifted, drifted, night by night,
  Craft that never shows a light;
Nor ever, to prevent worse knell,
Tolls in fog the warning bell.

From collision never shrinking,
Drive what may through darksome smother;
Saturate, but never sinking,
Fatal only to the *other!*
  Deadlier than the sunken reef
Since still the snare it shifteth,
  Torpid in dumb ambuscade
Waylayingly it drifteth.

              O, the sailors—O, the sails!
              O, the lost crews never heard of!
              Well the harp of Ariel wails
              Thoughts that tongue can tell no word of!

FAR OFF-SHORE.

Look, the raft, a signal flying,
  Thin—a shred;
None upon the lashed spars lying,
  Quick or dead.

Cries the sea-fowl, hovering over,
  "Crew, the crew?"
And the billow, reckless rover,
  Sweeps anew!

THE TUFT OF KELP.

All dripping in tangles green,
  Cast up by a lonely sea,
If purer for that, O Weed,
  Bitterer, too, are ye?

THE MALDIVE SHARK.

About the Shark, phlegmatical one,
Pale sot of the Maldive sea,
The sleek little pilot-fish, azure and slim,
How alert in attendance be.
From his saw-pit of mouth, from his charnel of maw
They have nothing of harm to dread,
But liquidly glide on his ghastly flank
Or before his Gorgonian head;
Or lurk in the port of serrated teeth
In white triple tiers of glittering gates,
And there find a haven when peril's abroad,
An asylum in jaws of the Fates!
They are friends; and friendly they guide him to prey,
Yet never partake of the treat—
Eyes and brains to the dotard lethargic and dull,
Pale ravener of horrible meat.

THE BERG.

(A Dream.)

I saw a ship of martial build
(Her standards set, her brave apparel on)
Directed as by madness mere
Against a stolid iceberg steer,
Nor budge it, though the infatuate ship went down.
The impact made huge ice-cubes fall
Sullen, in tons that crashed the deck;
But that one avalanche was all—
No other movement save the foundering wreck.

Along the spurs of ridges pale,
Not any slenderest shaft and frail,
A prism over glass-green gorges lone,
Toppled; nor lace of traceries fine,
Nor pendant drops in grot or mine
Were jarred, when the stunned ship went down.
Nor sole the gulls in cloud that wheeled
Circling one snow-flanked peak afar,
But nearer fowl the floes that skimmed
And crystal beaches, felt no jar.
No thrill transmitted stirred the lock
Of jack-straw needle-ice at base;
Towers undermined by waves—the block
Atilt impending—kept their place.
Seals, dozing sleek on sliddery ledges
Slipt never, when by loftier edges
Through very inertia overthrown,
The impetuous ship in bafflement went down.

Hard Berg (methought), so cold, so vast,
With mortal damps self-overcast;
Exhaling still thy dankish breath—
Adrift dissolving, bound for death;
Though lumpish thou, a lumbering one—

A lumbering lubbard loitering slow,
Impingers rue thee and go down,
Sounding thy precipice below,
Nor stir the slimy slug that sprawls
Along thy dead indifference of walls.

THE ENVIABLE ISLES.

(*From* "Rammon.")

Through storms you reach them and from storms are free.
   Afar descried, the foremost drear in hue,
But, nearer, green; and, on the marge, the sea
   Makes thunder low and mist of rainbowed dew.

But, inland, where the sleep that folds the hills
A dreamier sleep, the trance of God, instills—
   On uplands hazed, in wandering airs aswoon,
Slow-swaying palms salute love's cypress tree
   Adown in vale where pebbly runlets croon
A song to lull all sorrow and all glee.

Sweet-fern and moss in many a glade are here,
   Where, strown in flocks, what cheek-flushed myriads lie
Dimpling in dream—unconscious slumberers mere,
   While billows endless round the beaches die.

PEBBLES.

I.

Though the Clerk of the Weather insist,
  And lay down the weather-law,
Pintado and gannet they wist
That the winds blow whither they list
  In tempest or flaw.

II.

Old are the creeds, but stale the schools,
  Revamped as the mode may veer.
But Orm from the schools to the beaches strays,
And, finding a Conch hoar with time, he delays
  And reverent lifts it to ear.
That Voice, pitched in far monotone,
  Shall it swerve? shall it deviate ever?
The Seas have inspired it, and Truth—
  Truth, varying from sameness never.

III.

In hollows of the liquid hills
  Where the long Blue Ridges run,
The flattery of no echo thrills,
  For echo the seas have none;
Nor aught that gives man back man's strain—
The hope of his heart, the dream in his brain.

IV.

On ocean where the embattled fleets repair,
Man, suffering inflictor, sails on sufferance there.

V.

Implacable I, the old implacable Sea:
  Implacable most when most I smile serene—
Pleased, not appeased, by myriad wrecks in me.

VI.

Curled in the comb of yon billow Andean,
   Is it the Dragon's heaven-challenging crest?
Elemental mad ramping of ravening waters—
   Yet Christ on the Mount, and the dove in her nest!

VII.

Healed of my hurt, I laud the inhuman Sea—
Yea, bless the Angels Four that there convene;
For healed I am even by their pitiless breath
Distilled in wholesome dew named rosmarine.

BILLY IN THE DARBIES: from BILLY BUDD

Good of the Chaplain to enter Lone Bay
And down on his marrow-bones here and pray
For the likes just o' me, Billy Budd.—But look:
Through the port comes the moon-shine astray!
It tips the guard's cutlass and silvers this nook;
But 'twill die in the dawning of Billy's last day.
A jewel-block they'll make of me tomorrow,
Pendant pearl from the yard-arm-end
Like the ear-drop I gave to Bristol Molly—
O, 'tis me, not the sentence they'll suspend.
Ay, Ay, all is up; and I must up too
Early in the morning, aloft from alow.
On an empty stomach, now, never it would do.
They'll give me a nibble—bit o' biscuit ere I go.
Sure, a messmate will reach me the last parting cup;
But, turning heads away from the hoist and the belay,
Heaven knows who will have the running of me up!
No pipe to those halyards.—But aren't it all sham?
A blur's in my eyes; it is dreaming that I am.
A hatchet to my hawser? All adrift to go?
The drum roll to grog, and Billy never know?
But Donald he has promised to stand by the plank;
So I'll shake a friendly hand ere I sink.
But—no! It is dead then I'll be, come to think.—
I remember Taff the Welshman when he sank.
And his cheek it was like the budding pink[.]
But me they'll lash in hammock, drop me deep.
Fathoms down, fathoms down, how I'll dream fast asleep.
I feel it stealing now. Sentry, are you there?
Just ease these darbies at the wrist, and roll me over fair,
I am sleepy, and the oozy weeds about me twist.

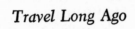

Travel Long Ago

TIMOLEON.

(394 B.C.)

I.

If more than once, as annals tell,
Through blood without compunction spilt,
An egotist arch rule has snatched
And stamped the seizure with his sabre's hilt,
   And, legalized by lawyers, stood;
Shall the good heart whose patriot fire
Leaps to a deed of startling note,
Do it, then flinch? Shall good in weak expire?
   Needs goodness lack the evil grit
That stares down censorship and ban,
And dumfounds saintlier ones with this—
God's will avouched in each successful man?
   Or, put it, where dread stress inspires
A virtue beyond man's standard rate,
Seems virtue there a strain forbid—
Transcendence such as shares transgression's fate?
   If so, and wan eclipse ensue,
Yet glory await emergence won,
Is that high Providence, or Chance?
And proved it which with thee, Timoleon?
   O, crowned with laurel twined with thorn,
Not rash thy life's cross-tide I stem,
But reck the problem rolled in pang
And reach and dare to touch thy garment's hem.

II.

   When Argos and Cleone strove
Against free Corinth's claim or right,
Two brothers battled for her well:
A footman one, and one a mounted knight.

Apart in place, each braved the brunt
Till the rash cavalryman, alone,
Was wrecked against the enemy's files,
His bayard crippled and he maimed and thrown.
　　Timoleon, at Timophanes' need,
Makes for the rescue through the fray,
Covers him with his shield, and takes
The darts and furious odds and fights at bay;
　　Till, wrought to palor of passion dumb,
Stark terrors of death around he throws,
Warding his brother from the field
Spite failing friends dispersed and rallying foes.
　　Here might he rest, in claim rest here,
Rest, and a Phidian form remain;
But life halts never, life must on,
And take with term prolonged some scar or stain.
　　Yes, life must on. And latent germs
Time's seasons wake in mead and man;
And brothers, playfellows in youth,
Develop into variance wide in span.

III.

　　Timophanes was his mother's pride—
Her pride, her pet, even all to her
Who slackly on Timoleon looked:
Scarce he (she mused) may proud affection stir.
　　He saved my darling, gossips tell:
If so, 'twas service, yea, and fair;
But instinct ruled and duty bade,
In service such, a henchman e'en might share.
　　When boys they were I helped the bent;
I made the junior feel his place,
Subserve the senior, love him, too;
And sooth he does, and that's his saving grace.
　　But me the meek one never can serve,
Not he, he lacks the quality keen
To make the mother through the son
An envied dame of power, a social queen.

But thou, my first-born, thou art I
In sex translated; joyed, I scan
My features, mine, expressed in thee;
Thou art what I would be were I a man.
  My brave Timophanes, 'tis thou
Who yet the world's fore-front shalt win,
For thine the urgent resolute way,
Self pushing panoplied self through thick and thin.
  Nor here maternal insight erred:
Foresworn, with heart that did not wince
At slaying men who kept their vows,
Her darling strides to power, and reigns—a Prince.

IV.

Because of just heart and humane,
Profound the hate Timoleon knew
For crimes of pride and men-of-prey
And impious deeds that perjurous upstarts do;
  And Corinth loved he, and in way
Old Scotia's clansman loved his clan,
Devotion one with ties how dear
And passion that late to make the rescue ran.
  But crime and kin—the terrorized town,
The silent, acquiescent mother—
Revulsion racks the filial heart,
The loyal son, the patriot true, the brother.
  In evil visions of the night
He sees the lictors of the gods,
Giant ministers of righteousness,
Their *fasces* threatened by the Furies' rods.
  But undeterred he wills to act,
Resolved thereon though Ate rise;
He heeds the voice whose mandate calls,
Or seems to call, peremptory from the skies.

V.

Nor less but by approaches mild,
And trying each prudential art,
The just one first advances him
In parley with a flushed intemperate heart.
　　The brother first he seeks—alone,
And pleads; but is with laughter met;
Then comes he, in accord with two,
And these adjure the tyrant and beset;
　　Whose merriment gives place to rage:
"Go," stamping, "what to me is Right?
I am the Wrong, and lo, I reign,
And testily intolerant too in might:"
　　And glooms on his mute brother pale,
Who goes aside; with muffled face
He sobs the predetermined word,
And Right in Corinth reassumes its place.

VI.

But on his robe, ah, whose the blood?
And craven ones their eyes avert,
And heavy is a mother's ban,
And dismal faces of the fools can hurt.
　　The whispering-gallery of the world,
Where each breathed slur runs wheeling wide
Eddies a false perverted truth,
Inveterate turning still on fratricide.
　　The time was Plato's. Wandering lights
Confirmed the atheist's standing star;
As now, no sanction Virtue knew
For deeds that on prescriptive morals jar.
　　Reaction took misgiving's tone,
Infecting conscience, till betrayed
To doubt the irrevocable doom
Herself had authorized when undismayed.
　　Within perturbed Timoleon here
Such deeps were bared as when the sea
Convulsed, vacates its shoreward bed,
And Nature's last reserves show nakedly.

He falters, and from Hades' glens
By night insidious tones implore—
Why suffer? hither come and be
What Phocion is who feeleth man no more.
      But, won from that, his mood elects
To live—to live in wilding place;
For years self-outcast, he but meets
In shades his playfellow's reproachful face.
      Estranged through one transcendent deed
From common membership in mart,
In severance he is like a head
Pale after battle trunkless found apart.

                    VII.

      But flood-tide comes though long the ebb,
Nor patience bides with passion long;
Like sightless orbs his thoughts are rolled
Arraigning heaven as compromised in wrong:
      To second causes why appeal?
Vain parleying here with fellow clods.
To you, Arch Principals, I rear
My quarrel, for this quarrel is with gods.
      Shall just men long to quit your world?
It is aspersion of your reign;
Your marbles in the temple stand—
Yourselves as stony and invoked in vain?
      Ah, bear with one quite overborne,
Olympians, if he chide ye now;
Magnanimous be even though he rail
And hard against ye set the bleaching brow.
      If conscience doubt, she'll next recant.
What basis then? O, tell at last,
Are earnest natures staggering here
But fatherless shadows from no substance cast?
      Yea, *are* ye, gods? Then ye, 'tis ye
Should show what touch of tie ye may,
Since ye, too, if not wrung are wronged
By grievous misconceptions of your sway.

But deign, some little sign be given—
Low thunder in your tranquil skies;
Me reassure, nor let me be
Like a lone dog that for a master cries.

VIII.

Men's moods, as frames, must yield to years,
And turns the world in fickle ways;
Corinth recalls Timoleon—ay,
And plumes him forth, but yet with schooling phrase.
    On Sicily's fields, through arduous wars,
A peace he won whose rainbow spanned
The isle redeemed; and he was hailed
Deliverer of that fair colonial land.
    And Corinth clapt: Absolved, and more!
Justice in long arrears is thine:
Not slayer of thy brother, no,
But savior of the state, Jove's soldier, man divine.
    Eager for thee thy City waits:
Return! with bays we dress your door.
But he, the Isle's loved guest, reposed,
And never for Corinth left the adopted shore.

AFTER THE PLEASURE PARTY.

LINES TRACED
UNDER AN IMAGE OF
AMOR THREATENING.

Fear me, virgin whosoever
Taking pride from love exempt,
    Fear me, slighted. Never, never
Brave me, nor my fury tempt:
Downy wings, but wroth they beat
Tempest even in reason's seat.

Behind the house the upland falls
With many an odorous tree—
White marbles gleaming through green halls,
Terrace by terrace, down and down,
And meets the starlit Mediterranean Sea.

'Tis Paradise. In such an hour
Some pangs that rend might take release.
Nor less perturbed who keeps this bower
Of balm, nor finds balsamic peace?
From whom the passionate words in vent
After long revery's discontent?

Tired of the homeless deep,
Look how their flight yon hurrying billows urge,
Hitherward but to reap
Passive repulse from the iron-bound verge!
Insensate, can they never know
'Tis mad to wreck the impulsion so?

An art of memory is, they tell:
But to forget! forget the glade
Wherein Fate sprung Love's ambuscade,
To flout pale years of cloistral life
And flush me in this sensuous strife.

'Tis Vesta struck with Sappho's smart.
No fable her delirious leap:
With more of cause in desperate heart,
Myself could take it—but to sleep!

Now first I feel, what all may ween,
That soon or late, if faded e'en,
One's sex asserts itself. Desire,
The dear desire through love to sway,
Is like the Geysers that aspire—
Through cold obstruction win their fervid way.
But baffled here—to take disdain,
To feel rule's instinct, yet not reign;
To dote, to come to this drear shame—
Hence the winged blaze that sweeps my soul
Like prairie fires that spurn control,
Where withering weeds incense the flame.

And kept I long heaven's watch for this,
Contemning love, for this, even this?
O terrace chill in Northern air,
O reaching ranging tube I placed
Against yon skies, and fable chased
Till, fool, I hailed for sister there
Starred Cassiopea in Golden Chair.
In dream I throned me, nor I saw
In cell the idiot crowned with straw.

And yet, ah yet scarce ill I reigned,
Through self-illusion self-sustained,
When now—enlightened, undeceived—
What gain I barrenly bereaved!
Than this can be yet lower decline—
Envy and spleen, can these be mine?

The peasant girl demure that trod
Beside our wheels that climbed the way,
And bore along a blossoming rod
That looked the sceptre of May-Day—
On her—to fire this petty hell,
His softened glance how moistly fell!

The cheat! on briars her buds were strung;
And wiles peeped forth from mien how meek.
The innocent bare-foot! young, so young!
To girls, strong man's a novice weak.
To tell such beads! And more remain,
Sad rosary of belittling pain.

When after lunch and sallies gay
Like the Decameron folk we lay
In sylvan groups; and I——let be!
O, dreams he, can he dream that one
Because not roseate feels no sun?
The plain lone bramble thrills with Spring
As much as vines that grapes shall bring.

Me now fair studies charm no more.
Shall great thoughts writ, or high themes sung
Damask wan cheeks—unlock his arm
About some radiant ninny flung?
How glad with all my starry lore,
I'd buy the veriest wanton's rose
Would but my bee therein repose.

Could I remake me! or set free
This sexless bound in sex, then plunge
Deeper than Sappho, in a lunge
Piercing Pan's paramount mystery!
For, Nature, in no shallow surge
Against thee either sex may urge,
Why hast thou made us but in halves—
Co-relatives? This makes us slaves.
If these co-relatives never meet
Self-hood itself seems incomplete.
And such the dicing of blind fate
Few matching halves here meet and mate.
What Cosmic jest or Anarch blunder
The human integral clove asunder
And shied the fractions through life's gate?

Ye stars that long your votary knew
Rapt in her vigil, see me here!
Whither is gone the spell ye threw

Old observance grave they offer;
But no Margrave fair,
In his living aspect gracious,
Sits responsive there;

No, and never guest once marvels,
None the good lord name,
Scarce they mark void throne and cover—
Dust upon the same.

Mindless as to what importeth
Absence such in hall;
Tacit as the plough-horse feeding
In the palfrey's stall.

Ah, enough for toil and travail,
If but for a night
Into wine is turned the water,
Black bread into white.

THE GARDEN OF METRODORUS.

The Athenians mark the moss-grown gate
And hedge untrimmed that hides the haven green:
   And who keeps here his quiet state?
   And shares he sad or happy fate
Where never foot-path to the gate is seen?

Here none come forth, here none go in,
Here silence strange, and dumb seclusion dwell:
   Content from loneness who may win?
   And is this stillness peace or sin
Which noteless thus apart can keep its dell?

IN A GARRET.

   Gems and jewels let them heap—
     Wax sumptuous as the Sophi:
   For me, to grapple from Art's deep
     One dripping trophy!

MONODY.

To have known him, to have loved him
   After loneness long;
And then to be estranged in life,
   And neither in the wrong;
And now for death to set his seal—
   Ease me, a little ease, my song!

By wintry hills his hermit-mound
   The sheeted snow-drifts drape,
And houseless there the snow-bird flits
   Beneath the fir-trees' crape:
Glazed now with ice the cloistral vine
   That hid the shyest grape.

LONE FOUNTS.

Though fast youth's glorious fable flies,
View not the world with worldling's eyes;
Nor turn with weather of the time.
Foreclose the coming of surprise:
Stand where Posterity shall stand;
Stand where the Ancients stood before,
And, dipping in lone founts thy hand,
Drink of the never-varying lore:
Wise once, and wise thence evermore.

THE BENCH OF BOORS.

In bed I muse on Tenier's boors,
Embrowned and beery losels all:
      A wakeful brain
      Elaborates pain:
Within low doors the slugs of boors
Laze and yawn and doze again.

In dreams they doze, the drowsy boors,
Their hazy hovel warm and small:
      Thought's ampler bound
      But chill is found:
Within low doors the basking boors
Snugly hug the ember-mound.

Sleepless, I see the slumberous boors
Their blurred eyes blink, their eyelids fall:
      Thought's eager sight
      Aches—overbright!
Within low doors the boozy boors
Cat-naps take in pipe-bowl light.

THE ENTHUSIAST.

"Though He slay me yet will I trust in Him."

Shall hearts that beat no base retreat
   In youth's magnanimous years—
Ignoble hold it, if discreet
   When interest tames to fears;
Shall spirits that worship light
   Perfidious deem its sacred glow,
   Recant, and trudge where worldlings go,
Conform and own them right?

Shall Time with creeping influence cold
   Unnerve and cow? the heart
Pine for the heartless ones enrolled
   With palterers of the mart?
Shall faith abjure her skies,
   Or pale probation blench her down
   To shrink from Truth so still, so lone
Mid loud gregarious lies?

Each burning boat in Cæsar's rear,
   Flames—No return through me!
So put the torch to ties though dear,
   If ties but tempters be.
Nor cringe if come the night:
   Walk through the cloud to meet the pall,
   Though light forsake thee, never fall
From fealty to light.

ART.

In placid hours well-pleased we dream
Of many a brave unbodied scheme.
But form to lend, pulsed life create,
What unlike things must meet and mate:
A flame to melt—a wind to freeze;
Sad patience—joyous energies;
Humility—yet pride and scorn;
Instinct and study; love and hate;
Audacity—reverence. These must mate,
And fuse with Jacob's mystic heart,
To wrestle with the angel—Art.

BUDDHA.

*"For what is your life? It is even a vapor that appeareth
for a little time and then vanisheth away."*

Swooning swim to less and less
    Aspirant to nothingness!
Sobs of the worlds, and dole of kinds
    That dumb endurers be—
Nirvana! absorb us in your skies,
    Annul us into thee.

FRAGMENTS OF A LOST GNOSTIC POEM OF THE 12TH CENTURY.

* * * *

Found a family, build a state,
The pledged event is still the same:
Matter in end will never abate
His ancient brutal claim.

* * * *

Indolence is heaven's ally here,
And energy the child of hell:
The Good Man pouring from his pitcher clear,
But brims the poisoned well.

THE MARCHIONESS OF BRINVILLIERS.

He toned the sprightly beam of morning
  With twilight meek of tender eve,
Brightness interfused with softness,
  Light and shade did weave:
And gave to candor equal place
With mystery starred in open skies;
And, floating all in sweetness, made
  Her fathomless mild eyes.

THE AGE OF THE ANTONINES.

While faith forecasts millenial years
Spite Europe's embattled lines,
Back to the Past one glance be cast—
   The Age of the Antonines!
O summit of fate, O zenith of time
When a pagan gentleman reigned,
And the olive was nailed to the inn of the world
Nor the peace of the just was feigned.
   A halcyon Age, afar it shines,
Solstice of Man and the Antonines.

Hymns to the nations' friendly gods
Went up from the fellowly shrines,
No demagogue beat the pulpit-drum
   In the Age of the Antonines!
The sting was not dreamed to be taken from death,
No Paradise pledged or sought,
But they reasoned of fate at the flowing feast,
Nor stifled the fluent thought.
   We sham, we shuffle while faith declines—
They were frank in the Age of the Antonines.

Orders and ranks they kept degree,
Few felt how the parvenu pines,
No law-maker took the lawless one's fee
   In the Age of the Antonines!
Under law made will the world reposed
And the ruler's right confessed,
For the heavens elected the Emperor then,
The foremost of men the best.
   Ah, might we read in America's signs
The Age restored of the Antonines.

HERBA SANTA.

I.

After long wars when comes release
Not olive wands proclaiming peace
  An import dearer share
Than stems of Herba Santa hazed
  In autumn's Indian air.
Of moods they breathe that care disarm,
They pledge us lenitive and calm.

II.

Shall code or creed a lure afford
To win all selves to Love's accord?
When Love ordained a supper divine
  For the wide world of man,
What bickerings o'er his gracious wine!
  Then strange new feuds began.

Effectual more in lowlier way,
  Pacific Herb, thy sensuous plea
The bristling clans of Adam sway
  At least to fellowship in thee!
Before thine altar tribal flags are furled,
Fain woulds't thou make one hearthstone of the world.

III.

To scythe, to sceptre, pen and hod—
  Yea, sodden laborers dumb;
To brains overplied, to feet that plod,
In solace of the *Truce of God*
  The Calumet has come!

IV.

Ah for the world ere Raleigh's find
  Never that knew this suasive balm
That helps when Gilead's fails to heal,
  Helps by an interserted charm.

Insinuous thou that through the nerve
  Windest the soul, and so canst win
  Some from repinings, some from sin,
The Church's aim thou dost subserve.

The ruffled fag fordone with care
  And brooding, Gold would ease this pain:
Him soothest thou and smoothest down
  Till some content return again.

Even ruffians feel thy influence breed
  Saint Martin's summer in the mind,
They feel this last evangel plead,
As did the first, apart from creed,
  Be peaceful, man—be kind!

V.

Rejected once on higher plain,
O Love supreme, to come again
  Can this be thine?
Again to come, and win us too
  In likeness of a weed
That as a god didst vainly woo,
  As man more vainly bleed?

VI.

Forbear, my soul! and in thine Eastern chamber
  Rehearse the dream that brings the long release:
Through jasmine sweet and talismanic amber
  Inhaling Herba Santa in the passive Pipe of Peace.

VENICE.

With Pantheist energy of will
The little craftsman of the Coral Sea
Strenuous in the blue abyss,
Up-builds his marvelous gallery
    And long arcade,
Erections freaked with many a fringe
    Of marble garlandry,
Evincing what a worm can do.

Laborious in a shallower wave,
    Advanced in kindred art,
A prouder agent proved Pan's might
When Venice rose in reefs of palaces.

IN A BYE-CANAL.

A swoon of noon, a trance of tide,
The hushed siesta brooding wide
 Like calms far off Peru;
No floating wayfarer in sight,
Dumb noon, and haunted like the night
 When Jael the wiled one slew.

A languid impulse from the oar
Plied by my indolent gondolier
Tinkles against a palace hoar,
 And, hark, response I hear!
A lattice clicks; and lo, I see
Between the slats, mute summoning me,
What loveliest eyes of scintillation,
What basilisk glance of conjuration!

 Fronted I have, part taken the span
Of portents in nature and peril in man.
I have swum—I have been
Twixt the whale's black flukes and the white shark's fin
The enemy's desert have wandered in,
And there have turned, have turned and scanned,
Following me how noiselessly,
Envy and Slander, lepers hand in hand.
All this. But at the latticed eye—
"Hey! Gondolier, you sleep, my man;
Wake up!" And, shooting by, we ran;
The while I mused, This, surely now,
Confutes the Naturalists, allow!
Sirens, true sirens verily be,
Sirens, waylayers in the sea.

Well, wooed by these same deadly misses,
Is it shame to run?
No! flee them did divine Ulysses,
 Brave, wise, and Venus' son.

PISA'S LEANING TOWER.

The Tower in tiers of architraves,
Fair circle over cirque,
A trunk of rounded colon[n]ades,
The maker's master-work,
Impends with all its pillared tribes,
And, poising them, debates:
It thinks to plunge—but hesitates;
Shrinks back—yet fain would slide;
Withholds itself—itself would urge;
Hovering, shivering on the verge,
    A would-be suicide!

IN A CHURCH OF PADUA.

In vaulted place where shadows flit,
An upright sombre box you see:
A door, but fast, and lattice none,
But punctured holes minutely small
In lateral silver panel square
Above a kneeling-board without,
Suggest an aim if not declare.

Who bendeth here the tremulous knee
No glimpse may get of him within,
And he immured may hardly see
The soul confessing there the sin;
Nor yields the low-sieved voice a tone
Whereby the murmurer may be known.

Dread diving-bell! In thee inurned
What hollows the priest must sound,
Descending into consciences
    Where more is hid than found.

MILAN CATHEDRAL.

Through light green haze, a rolling sea
Over gardens where redundance flows,
    The fat old plain of Lombardy,
The White Cathedral shows.

    Of Art the miracles
    Its tribes of pinnacles
Gleam like to ice-peaks snowed; and higher,
Erect upon each airy spire
    In concourse without end,
Statues of saints over saints ascend
Like multitudinous forks of fire.

What motive was the master-builder's here?
Why these synodic hierarchies given,
Sublimely ranked in marble sessions clear,
Except to signify the host of heaven.

THE PARTHENON.

I.

Seen aloft from afar.

Estranged in site,
Aerial gleaming, warmly white,
You look a suncloud motionless
In noon of day divine;
Your beauty charmed enhancement takes
In Art's long after-shine.

II.

Nearer viewed.

Like Lais, fairest of her kind,
In subtlety your form's defined—
The cornice curved, each shaft inclined,
While yet, to eyes that do but revel
   And take the sweeping view,
Erect this seems, and that a level,
   To line and plummet true.

Spinoza gazes; and in mind
Dreams that one architect designed
   Lais—and you!

III.

The Frieze.

What happy musings genial went
With airiest touch the chisel lent
   To frisk and curvet light
Of horses gay—their riders grave—
Contrasting so in action brave
   With virgins meekly bright,
Clear filing on in even tone
With pitcher each, one after one
   Like water-fowl in flight.

IV.

The last Tile.

When the last marble tile was laid
The winds died down on all the seas;
   Hushed were the birds, and swooned the glade;
   Ictinus sat; Aspasia said
"Hist!—Art's meridian, Pericles!"

GREEK MASONRY.

Joints were none that mortar sealed:
   Together, scarce with line revealed,
The blocks in symmetry congealed.

GREEK ARCHITECTURE.

Not magnitude, not lavishness,
   But Form—the Site;
Not innovating wilfulness,
   But reverence for the Archetype.

OFF CAPE COLONNA.

Aloof they crown the foreland lone,
  From aloft they loftier rise—
Fair columns, in the aureola rolled
  From sunned Greek seas and skies.
They wax, sublimed to fancy's view,
A god-like group against the blue.

Over much like gods! Serene they saw
  The wolf-waves board the deck,
And headlong hull of Falconer,
  And many a deadlier wreck.

THE APPARITION.

*(The Parthenon uplifted on
its rock first challenging the view
on the approach to Athens.)*

Abrupt the supernatural Cross,
  Vivid in startled air,
Smote the Emperor Constantine
And turned his soul's allegiance there.

With other power appealing down,
  Trophy of Adam's best!
If cynic minds you scarce convert,
You try them, shake them, or molest.

Diogenes, that honest heart,
  Lived ere your date began;
Thee had he seen, he might have swerved
In mood nor barked so much at Man.

THE ARCHIPELAGO.

Sail before the morning breeze
The Sporads through and Cyclades
They look like isles of absentees—
           Gone whither?

You bless Apollo's cheering ray,
But Delos, his own isle, today
Not e'en a Selkirk there to pray
           God friend me!

Scarce lone these groups, scarce lone and bare
When Theseus roved a Raleigh there,
Each isle a small Virginia fair—
           Unravished.

Nor less through havoc fell they rue,
They still retain in outline true
Their grace of form when earth was new
           And primal.

But beauty clear, the frame's as yet,
Never shall make one quite forget
Thy picture, Pan, therein once set—
           Life's revel!

'Tis Polynesia reft of palms,
Seaward no valley breathes her balms—
Not such as musk thy rings of calms,
           Marquesas!

IN THE DESERT.

Never Pharaoh's Night,
Whereof the Hebrew wizards croon,
Did so the Theban flamens try
As me this veritable Noon.

Like blank ocean in blue calm
Undulates the ethereal frame;
In one flowing oriflamme
God flings his fiery standard out.

Battling with the Emirs fierce
Napoleon a great victory won,
Through and through his sword did pierce;
But, bayonetted by this sun
His gunners drop beneath the gun.

Holy, holy, holy Light!
Immaterial incandescence,
Of God the effluence of the essence,
Shekinah intolerably bright!

Weeds, Wildings, and Roses

THE LITTLE GOOD FELLOWS

Make way, make way, give leave to rove
Under your orchard as above;
A yearly welcome if ye love!
And all who loved us alway[s] throve.

Love for love. For ever we
When some unfriended man we see
Lifeless under forest-eaves,
Cover him with buds and leaves;
And charge the chipmunk, mouse, and mole—
Molest not this poor human soul!

Then let us never on green floor
Where your paths wind round about,
Keep to the middle in misdoubt,
Shy and aloof, unsure of ye;
But come like grass to stones on moor,
Wherever mortals be.

But toss your caps, O maids and men,
Snow-bound long in farm-house pen:
We chase Old Winter back to den.
See our red waistcoats! Alive be then—
Alive to the bridal-favors when
They blossom your orchards every Spring,
And cock-robin curves on a bridegroom's wing.

CLOVER

The June day dawns, the joy-winds rush,
    Your jovial fields are dres[s]t;
Rosier for thee the Dawn's red flush,
    Ruddier the Ruddock's breast.

TROPHIES OF PEACE

ILLINOIS IN 1840

Files on files of Prairie Maize:
On hosts of spears the morning plays!
Aloft the rustling streamers show:
The floss embrowned is rich below.

When Asia scarfed in silks came on
Against the Greek at Marathon,
Did each plume and pennon dance
Sun-lit thus on helm and lance
Mindless of War's sickle so?

For them, a tasseled dance of death:
For these—the reapers reap them low.
Reap them low, and stack the plain
With Ceres' trophies, golden grain.

Such monuments, and only such,
O Prairie! termless yield,
Though trooper Mars disdainful flout
Nor Annals fame the field.

FIELD ASTERS

Like the stars in commons blue
Peep their namesakes, Asters here,
Wild ones every autumn seen—
Seen of all, arresting few.

Seen indeed. But who their cheer
Interpret may, or what they mean
When so inscrutably their eyes
Us star-gazers scrutinize.

THE AMERICAN ALOE ON EXHIBITION

It is but a floral superstition, as everybody knows, that this plant flowers only once in a century. When in any instance the flowering is for decades delayed beyond the normal period, (eight or ten years at furthest) it is owing to something retarding in the environment or soil.

But few they were who came to see
    The Century-Plant in flower:
Ten cents admission—price you pay
    For bon-bons of the hour.

In strange inert blank unconcern
    Of wild things at the Zoo,
The patriarch let the sight-seers stare—
    Nor recked who came to view.

But lone at night the garland sighed
    While moaned the aged stem:
"At last, at last! but joy and pride
    What part have I with them?

Let be the dearth that kept me back
    Now long from wreath decreed;
But, Ah, ye Roses that have passed
    Accounting me a weed![")]

ROSARY BEADS

The Accepted Time

Adore the Roses; nor delay
  Until the rose-fane fall,
Or ever their censers cease to sway:
  "To-day!" the rose-priests call.

Without Price

Have the Roses. Needs no pelf
  The blooms to buy,
Nor any rose-bed to thyself
  Thy skill to try:
But live up to the Rose's light,
Thy meat shall turn to roses red,
  Thy bread to roses white.

Grain by Grain

Grain by grain the Desert drifts
Against the Garden-Land:
Hedge well thy Roses, head the stealth
Of ever-creeping Land.

A Fate Subdued

IMMOLATED.

Children of my happier prime,
When One yet lived with me, and threw
Her rainbow over life and time,
Even Hope, my bride, and mother to you;
O, nurtured in sweet pastoral air,
And fed on flowers and light, and dew
Of morning meadows—spare, Ah, spare
Reproach; spare, and upbraid me not
That, yielding scarce to reckless mood
But jealous of your future lot,
I sealed you in a fate subdued.
Have I not saved you from the drear
Theft and ignoring which need be
The triumph of the insincere
Unanimous Mediocrity?
Rest therefore, free from all despite,
Snugged in the arms of comfortable night.

THE RUSTY MAN.

(By a timid one)

In La Mancha he mopeth
  With beard thin and dusty;
He doteth and mopeth
  In library fusty—
'Mong his old folios gropeth:
  Cites obsolete saws
  Of chivalry's laws—
  Be the wronged one's knight:
  Die, but do right.
So he rusts and musts,
While each grocer green
Thriveth apace with the fulsome face
Of a fool serene.

CAMOËNS.

1
(BEFORE)

Ever restless, restless, craving rest—
The Imperfect toward Perfection pressed!
Yea, for the God demands thy best.
The world with endless beauty teems,
And thought evokes new worlds of dreams:
Hunt then the flying herds of themes!
And fan, yet fan thy fervid fire,
Until the crucibled gold shall show
That fire can purge, as well as glow.
In ordered ardor, nobly strong,
Flame to the height of epic song.

Camoëns in the hospital

2
(AFTER)

What now avails the pageant verse,
Trophies and arms with music borne?
Base is the world; and some rehearse
How noblest meet ignoble scorn.
Vain now the ardor, vain thy fire,
Delirium mere, unsound desire:
Fate's knife hath ripped thy chorded lyre.
Exhausted by the exacting lay,
Thou dost but fall a surer prey
To wile and guile ill understood;
While they who work them, fair in face,
Still keep their strength in prudent place,
And claim they worthier run life's race,
Serving high God with useful good.

A REASONABLE CONSTITUTION.

What though Reason forged your scheme?
'Twas Reason dreamed the Utopia's dream:
'Tis dream to think that Reason can
Govern the reasoning creature, man.

MONTAIGNE AND HIS KITTEN.

Hither, Blanche! 'Tis you and I.
Now that not a fool is by
To say we fool it—let us fool!
We, you know, in mind are one,
Alumni of no fagging school;
Superfluous business still we shun;
And ambition we let go,
The while poor dizzards strain and strive,
Rave and slave, drudge and drive,
Chasing ever, to and fro,
After ends that seldom gain
Scant exemption from life's pain.

But preachment proses, and so I.
Blanche, round your furred neck let me tie
This Order, with brave rib[b]on, see,—
The King he pinned it upon me.

But hark ye, sweeting,—well-a-day!
Forever shall ye purr this way—
Forever comfortable be?
Don't you wish now 'twas for ye,
Our grandiose eternity?
Pish! what fops we humans here,
Won't admit within our sphere
The whitest doe, nor even thee—
We, the spotless humans, we!

Preaching, prosing—scud and run,
Earnestness is far from fun.
Bless me, Blanche; we'll frisk to-night,
Hearts be ours lilt and light—
Gambol, skip, and frolic, play:
Wise ones fool it while they may!

HEARTS-OF-GOLD.

Pity, if true,
What the pewterer said—
Hearts-of-gold be few.
Howbeit, when snug in my bed,
And the fire-light flickers and yellows,
I dream of the hearts-of-gold sped—
The Falernian fellows—
Hafiz and Horace,
And Beranger—all
Dexterous tumblers eluding the Fall,
Fled? can be sped?
But the marygold's morris
Is danced o'er their head;
But their memory mellows,
Embalmed and becharmed,
Hearts-of-gold and good fellows!

PONTOOSUCE.

Crowning a bluff where gleams the lake below,
Some pillared pines in well-spaced order stand
And like an open temple show.
And here in best of seasons bland,
Autumnal noon-tide, I look out
From dusk arcades on sunshine all about.

Beyond the Lake, in upland cheer
Fields, pastoral fields, and barns appear,
They skirt the hills where lonely roads
Revealed in links thro' tiers of woods
Wind up to indistinct abodes
And faery-peopled neighborhoods;
While further fainter mountains keep
Hazed in romance impenetrably deep.

Look, corn in stacks, on many a farm,
And orchards ripe in languorous charm,
As dreamy Nature, feeling sure
Of all her genial labor done,
And the last mellow fruitage won,
Would idle out her term mature;
Reposing like a thing reclined
In kinship with man's meditative mind.

For me, within the brown arcade—
Rich life, methought; sweet here in shade
And pleasant abroad in air!—But, nay,
A counter thought intrusive played,
A thought as old as thought itself,
And who shall lay it on the shelf!—
I felt the beauty bless the day
In opulence of autumn's dower;
But evanescence will not stay!
A year ago was such an hour,
As this, which but foreruns the blast
Shall sweep these live leaves to the dead leaves past.

All dies!—

I stood in revery long.
Then, to forget death's ancient wrong,
I turned me in the brown arcade,
And there by chance in lateral glade
I saw low tawny mounds in lines
Relics of trunks of stately pines
Ranked erst in colonnades where, lo!
Erect succeeding pillars show!

All dies! and not alone
The aspiring trees and men and grass;
The poet's forms of beauty pass,
And noblest deeds they are undone.

All dies!

The workman dies, and after him, the work;
Like to these pines whose graves I trace,
Statue and statuary fall upon their face:
In very amaranths the worm doth lurk,
Even stars, Chaldæans say, fade from the starry space.
Andes and Apalachee tell
Of havoc ere our Adam fell,
And present Nature as a moss doth show
On the ruins of the Nature of the æons of long ago.

But look—and hark!

Adown the glade,
Where light and shadow sport at will,
Who cometh vocal, and arrayed
As in the first pale tints of morn—
So pure, rose-clear, and fresh and chill!
Some ground-pine sprigs her brow adorn,
The earthy rootlets tangled clinging.
Over tufts of moss which dead things made,
Under vital twigs which danced or swayed,
Along she floats, and lightly singing:

"Dies, all dies!
The grass it dies, but in vernal rain
Up it springs and it lives again;
Over and over, again and again
It lives, it dies and it lives again.
Who sighs that all dies?
Summer and winter, and pleasure and pain
And everything everywhere in God's reign,
They end, and anon they begin again:
Wane and wax, wax and wane:
Over and over and over amain
End, ever end, and begin again—
End, ever end, and forever and ever begin again!"

She ceased, and nearer slid, and hung
In dewy guise; then softlier sung:
"Since light and shade are equal set
And all revolves, nor more ye know;
Ah, why should tears the pale cheek fret
For aught that waneth here below.
Let go, let go!"

With that, her warm lips thrilled me through,
She kissed me, while her chaplet cold
Its rootlets brushed against my brow
With all their humid clinging mould.
She vanished, leaving fragrant breath
And warmth and chill of wedded life and death.

Comment on the Poems

The Civil War

MELVILLE'S PREFACE AND DEDICATION

Melville dedicated *Battle-Pieces* to the "three hundred thousand who in the war for the maintenance of the Union fell devotedly under the flag of their fathers." He also provided the following prefatory note:

> With few exceptions, the Pieces in this volume originated in an impulse imparted by the fall of Richmond. They were composed without reference to collective arrangement, but, being brought together in review, naturally fall into the order assumed.
> The events and incidents of the conflict—making up a whole, in varied amplitude, corresponding with the geographical area covered by the war—from these but a few themes have been taken, such as for any cause chanced to imprint themselves upon the mind.
> The aspects which the strife as a memory assumes are as manifold as are the moods of involuntary meditation—moods variable, and at times widely at variance. Yielding instinctively, one after another, to feelings not inspired from any one source exclusively, and unmindful, without purposing to be, of consistency, I seem, in most of these verses, to have but placed a harp in a window, and noted the contrasted airs which wayward winds have played upon the strings.

THE PORTENT   [page 2]

John Brown was hanged on December 2, 1859, following his conviction on charges of treason and inciting slaves to commit treason and murder, which arose from his attack of the previous October 16 on the United States Arsenal at Harper's Ferry, Virginia.

The form of the poem is shaped by the image of Brown's body as it sways rhythmically from the gallows and by a double refrain which plays the words "Shenandoah" and "John Brown" against each other. The Shenandoah Valley, of legendary beauty and fertility, was to be the scene of important military operations, including Union General Philip Sheridan's systematic campaign of devastation. As it stands in contrast to the greenness of the valley, the name "John Brown" suggests death. Brown is "weird" in the sense that his behavior was strange and his physical appearance peculiar, especially with beard streaming from beneath the covering that the hangman had placed over his face. But the word also emphasizes his prophetic role, calling to mind the Weird Sisters or Fates of Germanic mythology and the traditional superstitions associated with meteors. The phrase, "cut is on the crown," refers to a head wound which Brown received when he was captured, but it also suggests that the State itself has been endangered.

MISGIVINGS [page 3]

The storm of "autumn brown" sweeping into the peaceful valley fulfills the dire predictions of "The Portent" and recalls John Brown's shadow over the Shenandoah. The church spire, emblem of religious authority, cannot withstand the storm, itself an emblem of the dark forces of Nature and a portent of further storms.

THE CONFLICT OF CONVICTIONS [page 4]

The gloomy lull of the early part of the winter of 1860–1, seeming big with final disaster to our institutions, affected some minds that believed them to constitute one of the great hopes of mankind, much as the eclipse which came over the promise of the first French Revolution affected kindred natures, throwing them for the time into doubts and misgivings universal.

(*Melville's Note*)

The influence of Milton's *Paradise Lost* on this poem is seen in its theme, setting, imagery, and many of its allusions. *Paradise Lost* concerns man's initial fall from grace; "The Conflict of Convictions" deals with "man's latter fall." By presenting the Civil War in the context of the War in Heaven, Melville clarifies and enhances its significance and at the same time recognizes it as another episode in the eternal conflict between good and evil. The title of the poem refers to the antagonisms of the coming war and to the structure of the poem which consists of seven irregular stanzas, each with its chorus. The stanzas function as stages in a debate, alternating between a negative pessimism and qualified optimism. A tentative hopefulness appears in the last stanza arising from the possibility that "the Iron Dome," symbol of the State, might emerge stronger from the strain of the conflict. The final chorus, however, emphasizes the disinterest of God in the partisan struggles of man.

"Prophesy," in the last line, is Melville's spelling.

APATHY AND ENTHUSIASM   [page 7]

The source of this poem, including its Easter imagery, is probably an editorial from the New York *Times* of April 16, 1861, "The Resurrection of Patriotism," as reprinted in *The Rebellion Record*, a periodical which systematically published official reports, newspaper dispatches, verse, and anecdotes from both sides. The bound files of eight of the eleven volumes (1860–63) were available when Melville was writing *Battle-Pieces* and he drew upon them for at least twenty of the war poems.

Once again Melville sets up thematic oppositions—death and resurrection, winter and spring, dejection and elation, age and youth, doubt and faith, Michael and Satan—and uses them to inform his poem.

THE MARCH INTO VIRGINIA   [page 9]

On July 21, 1861, at Bull Run near Manassas Junction, Virginia, Confederate forces under General P. G. T. Beauregard defeated a larger Federal army under General Irvin McDowell in the first important battle of the Civil War. The following summer the Confederates were again victorious in a major engagement at Manassas, August 29–30, 1862.

The poem is concerned with the experience of initiation. Picnic grounds become battlefields as the "boys" become sacrificial victims of Moloch, who required children to be passed through fire to him. Some of the "boys," as they march blithely "in lightsome files" to battle, will be "enlightened" by the volleys of gunfire, which are capable literally and figuratively of producing light. The survivors, matured by the experience of battle, must yet endure the augmented shame and agony of further defeat by the same foe on the same field, in the Second Battle of Manassas. Cf. "The Fortitude of the North."

BALL'S BLUFF   [page 11]

On October 21, 1861, Colonel Edward D. Baker, senator from Oregon and friend of Lincoln, led a disastrous raid against Confederate positions on the Potomac River near Ball's Bluff, Virginia. Baker was ambushed but fought bravely until he was killed. Recriminations followed, including charges of treason, political interference with military operations, and wanton waste of lives.

Melville again establishes contrasts: noon and night, elation and sobriety, life and death, action and thought, and the irony of the "brave boys" asleep beneath the cliffs of the Potomac while the wakeful poet muses on his memories of them. The sounds of the fifes and the cheering with which the poem begins decline into the distant sound of footsteps which have "died away."

DUPONT'S ROUND FIGHT   [page 12]

The Union fleet under the command of Commodore Samuel Francis Du Pont, reduced the Confederate forts guarding opposite shores of Port Royal Sound, South Carolina, on November 7, 1861, thereby obtaining a base for the subsequent coastal blockade and other important operations. A description and drawing of the "Plan of the Battle of Port Royal, S.C." published in *The Rebellion Record* (III, 106) is Melville's source and provided his mathematical and astronomical imagery. The caption accompanying the drawing reads: "The plan of attack was simple and effective, being for the ships to steam in a circle, or ellipse, running close to one shore as they came *down* the river, drifting or steaming as slowly as possible past the batteries there, and paying their fiery respects, and then making the turn to go back, and as they went *up* the river, favoring the other batteries with a similar compliment." Cf. circle and orbit imagery in *Pierre*.

The poem is a notable expression of Melville's aesthetic and its underlying philosophical assumptions. Social and artistic accomplishment, like victory in a naval battle, the stars in the heavens, and the propositions of geometry, depend upon ethically derived laws.

IN THE TURRET   [page 13]

On March 8, 1862, the Confederate ironclad *Merrimac* rammed and sank the wooden man-of-war *Cumberland* in Chesapeake Bay near Newport News, Virginia. On the following day the Union ironclad *Monitor*, commanded by Lieutenant John Lorimer Worden, arrived to do battle. Neither ironclad could destroy the other, and while the *Merrimac* did not attack the Union fleet again, she prevented McClellan's army from receiving adequate naval support.

Like Alcides, another name for Hercules, Worden was capable of descending into Hell if necessary. Through the new technology that produced the ironclad, he is able to penetrate to great depths but he is "cribbed" or confined by his "craft," a word used in the double sense of vessel and limitations of technical skill. The "spirit" that warns and derides Worden before the battle increases the horror of his unusual situation. The warning may also refer to the eye injury that Worden was to sustain as well as to the "goblin-snare" that the new technology represents. Worden's success derives from his staunch sense of duty and his ability, despite the injury to his sight, to see the full implication of the technology that he serves and that serves him. Thus he could fight effectively and survive the battle and the ultimate destruction of the *Monitor*, which went down in a storm off Cape Hatteras.

THE TEMERAIRE   [page 15]

The *Temeraire*, that storied ship of the old English fleet, and the subject of the well-known painting by Turner, commends itself to the mind seeking for some one craft to stand for the poetic ideal of those great historic wooden warships, whose gradual displacement is lamented by none more than by regularly educated navy officers, and of all nations.

(*Melville's Note*)

Melville saw "The Fighting *Temeraire*" by J. M. W. Turner in 1857 when he visited the National Gallery in London. The famous painting suggested to him the image of the decayed majesty of the anchored fleet of wooden ships at sunset, with which the poem begins, and the tugboat near the end. Turner's painting, "The Angel in the Sun," also in the National Gallery, as well as the Bible (Revelation 10:1) and Milton (*Paradise Lost*, III, 622–23) may lie behind the allusion in the last line of stanza four. Robert Southey's *Life of Nelson* was the source of the reference to the *Victory*, Admiral Nelson's flagship at the Battle of Trafalgar; to Nelson, with decorations shining on his frock coat, exposing his person to enemy fire; and to the four ships grappled together in deadly battle.

Much concerned with the significance of symbols, Melville found the erosion of meaningfulness from nautical "emblazonment" and "heraldry" poignant but appropriate. He annotated the word "Armorial" as follows:

> Some of the cannon of old times, especially the brass ones, unlike the more effective ordnance of the present day, were cast in shapes which Cellini might have designed, were gracefully enchased, generally with the arms of the country. A few of them—field-pieces—captured in our earlier wars, are preserved in arsenals and navy-yards.

A UTILITARIAN VIEW OF THE MONITOR'S FIGHT [page 17]

The implications of the inconclusive engagement between the Union ironclad *Monitor* and the Confederate *Merrimac* at Hampton Roads, Virginia, on March 9, 1862, were important to Melville who had served some nineteen years before as an ordinary seaman in the United States Navy. He was aware that the nature of war had changed, that the "martial utilitarians," to use his phrase from *Billy Budd*, would supplant the epic heroes of the days of oaken ships. He felt that poets should adopt a style and forms appropriate to the conflicts of "artisans" and "operatives," latter-day warriors who win battles by their "calculations of caloric." Melville seems to regret the change but to sense that the outward appearance of war is now more suitable to its true nature, purged as it is of a false rhetoric. His deliberate attempt to suit form to content is notably successful. For example, the heavy beat of the rhythm suggests the pounding of machinery and the run-on lines the relentless onward motion of mechanized propulsion. Rhyme is minimal, sound effects generally harsh and nervous, vocabulary heavily technological, and imagery derived largely from mechanistic devices or soiled, discarded military trappings.

SHILOH [page 18]

The bloody but indecisive Battle of Shiloh on April 6–7, 1862, near Pittsburg Landing, Tennessee, was the second major engagement of the Civil War. Melville appears to have drawn on *The Rebellion Record* (IV, 356–417) for the solacing rain, the log church, and other details. He changed the day of the fight at the church from Monday to Sunday to heighten the sense of profanation.

The structure of the poem is circular, a counterpart of the wheeling swallows at the beginning and end of what is grammatically a single sentence. The swallows seem consolatory, suggesting that Nature survives while men, in their deception, kill each other and are "undeceived" only in death.

MALVERN HILL [page 19]

The last of the Seven Days' Battles, Malvern Hill, on July 1, 1862, marked the end of General George B. McClellan's unsuccessful Peninsular Campaign against Richmond.

A newspaper dispatch reprinted in *The Rebellion Record* (V, 266) mentions a "fine grove of ancient elms" at Malvern Hill which in their serenity "seemed a bitter satire on the wickedness of man," and Melville may have paid particular attention to these trees when he visited the battlefield in April 1864. Like the image of the swallows in the poem, "Shiloh," the elms provide a structural framework and symbolize the order of Nature as opposed to the chaos and transience of man. They represent a fundamental sense of proportion as they answer the sequence of questions concerning the memorability of the fierce battle fought in their shade.

BATTLE OF STONE RIVER, TENNESSEE
[page 21]

The Battle of Stones River or Murfreesboro, Tennessee, was fought vigorously for four days beginning on December 30, 1862, between the Union Army of the Cumberland under General William S. Rosecrans and the Confederate Army of Tennessee under Generals Braxton Bragg and John C. Breckinridge. Tactically, it ended in a draw.

In this poem Melville places the Civil War in the larger context of history, obtaining through a comparison with the Wars of the Roses a sense of perspective similar to that which he found in Nature as represented by the elms of "Malvern Hill" and the swallows of "Shiloh." At Barnet Heath on April 14, 1471, an Easter morning, Edward IV of York defeated the Lancastrian army. He completed his victory and ended the civil Wars of the Roses at Tewkesbury the following May 3. The sacrilege of fratricidal strife is emphasized in the second stanza by the bitter wit of the wordplay and religious imagery.

Each of the four stanzas carries an incremental refrain, alternately a statement and a question relating to the possibility of reconciling the civil conflict. That the poem ends with a question suggests that Melville felt a reconciliation would be difficult.

In his travel journal of May 3, 1857, Melville described the "Oxford cloisters" as the "Most interesting spot I have seen in England." He was much impressed by the "tranquility & beauty" of the natural setting, which seemed to him remote from "all the violence of revolutions. &c."

STONEWALL JACKSON   [page 23]

General Thomas J. Jackson was fatally wounded on May 2, 1863, at Chancellorsville, Virginia, by fire from a Confederate outpost which, in the dusk and tangled forest, mistook him and his staff for Federal cavalry. Melville made Jackson the subject of a second poem in *Battle-Pieces* and expressed regard for him in the "Supplement" essay in the same book. He represented for Melville the complexity of the issues, the valor, and the degrees of rectitude and error of both North and South which made partisan judgment of the war all but impossible.

THE HOUSE-TOP   [page 24]

Federal troops were called in to put down the draft riots that broke out in New York on July 11, 1863, following the publication of a list of those called into military service. The rioters attacked Negroes and burned a Negro orphanage and church. Casualties approached a thousand and much property was lost through looting and arson.

To Melville this disgraceful episode was a reminder of the jungle beast in man which required the restraint of the harsh laws of Draco and the severe creed of Calvin, "civil charms" and "priestly spells," even "cynic tyrannies of honest kings," if man were to be saved from the dangers of degeneration. (For pertinent implications of the word "cynic," see the Comment, p. 248, on "The Apparition.") He annotated the line "And man rebounds whole aeons back in nature" as follows: " 'I dare not write the horrible and inconceivable atrocities committed,' says Froissart, in alluding to the remarkable sedition in France during his time. The like may be hinted of some proceedings of the draft-riotors."

Melville doubted the doctrine of the natural goodness of man and saw its acceptance as a danger to the Republic, whose citizens—unlike the apostle Paul, who invoked his right as a Roman to be exempt from the scourge—at least metaphorically needed a taste of the whip from time to time.

THE ARMIES OF THE WILDERNESS   [page 25]

The Wilderness, a large forest of second-growth timber south of the Rapidan River in Spotsylvania County, Virginia, was the scene of an engagement beginning on May 5, 1864, between the Army of the Potomac commanded by Grant and the Army of Northern Virginia under Lee. The fighting was prolonged, bitter, and inconclusive.

Almost exactly a year before, the Battle of Chancellorsville took place in the same forest. While Melville focuses on the Battle of the Wilderness, he refers to both engagements and encompasses both in the dates which form part of the title. Allusions to biblical wildernesses as places of suffering and mystery add to the richness of the poem's implications. Like "The Conflict of Convictions," each stanza includes a terse chorus. The stanzas depict specific events in the loose narrative and the choruses provide a commentary. As he indicates in the last stanza, Melville used "entangled rhyme" to parallel the ambiguity of the wilderness setting and the "riddle" that was posed there.

ON THE PHOTOGRAPH OF A CORPS COMMANDER   [page 32]

The Spotsylvania, Virginia, battle of May 12, 1864, was part of the Wilderness Campaign. Among the corps commanders who took part, General Winfield Scott Hancock of the II Corps, achieved the greatest distinction. His most notable feat was the capture of a large part of the Confederate "Stonewall" Brigade.

Melville's theme is the nature of leadership. He develops it by manipulating the word "man" and its cognates, "manly," "manhood," "fellow-man," and "men." The manly leader is both inspiration and catalyst. Because he is merely a man he can draw together his fellow men into a bond of brotherhood in a manner that not even God, who overawes man, can accomplish. In so doing he decreases the dangers to which he is subject as an individual exalted above his fellows.

SHERIDAN AT CEDAR CREEK   [page 33]

Confederate forces under General Jubal Early were successful in the memorable Battle of Cedar Creek, Virginia,

October 19, 1864, until General Philip Sheridan arrived after a hard ride from Winchester, fourteen miles away, to conduct a counterattack.

When first published in *Harper's New Monthly Magazine* for April 1866, the poem had the title "Philip," a hint of the epic role in which Melville saw Sheridan. Melville seems to have been thinking of classical battles and odes. He pays Sheridan the higher compliment of praising his horse and his soldiers, thereby investing him with an aura of kingly dignity. Unfortunately, he could not resist wordplay on Early's name in a stanza notable for other examples of reversal appropriate to the change in fortune accomplished by Sheridan's ride.

THE COLLEGE COLONEL [page 35]

Melville was living in Pittsfield, Massachusetts, in August 1863, when that town honored the 49th Regiment and its colonel, William Francis Bartlett. There was a parade and fireworks, and the Melville house was among those decked with flags and festoons. Colonel Bartlett left Harvard to enlist as a private. He was commissioned a captain in the 20th Massachusetts, lost a leg in the Peninsular Campaign, and was mustered out of the service in November 1862. He then organized and commanded a regiment, was twice wounded at Port Hudson, Louisiana, and again in the Wilderness fighting. As a brigadier general, he fought at the Battle of the Crater, at Petersburg, Virginia, July 30, 1864, was captured, and taken to Richmond. Melville presented him with a copy of *Battle-Pieces*. He is the archetype of the boyish soldiers "enlightened by the vollied glare" in "The March into Virginia."

AT THE CANNON'S MOUTH [page 36]

Lieutenant William B. Cushing and a volunteer crew sank the Confederate ironclad ram *Albemarle* at its heavily protected anchorage in the Roanoke River near Plymouth, North Carolina, on October 27, 1864. The ram had done much damage to the Federal fleet and a new attack from it was anticipated. Cushing used a steam launch to which was attached a spar-torpedo. Of the crew of fifteen, only he and one other man escaped death or capture.

The twenty-one-year-old Cushing is associated with the handsome youth Adonis who rejected the blandishments of Venus to hunt the wild boar. His motivation is as mysterious and "unfathomable" as that of the beautiful poisoner in the poem, "The Marchioness of Brinvilliers," and whatever motivates both is expressed by Melville through similar references to the depth of their eyes. Cushing's feat is crowned with success because he scorns success and is concerned with the deed itself.

THE MARCH TO THE SEA   [page 37]

After the burning of Atlanta on November 15, 1864, Sherman began his March to the Sea. His object was to take Savannah, but he sought to mislead the Confederate forces by diversionary feints. On December 10 he invested Savannah, splitting the Confederacy and re-establishing his communications with the North. Most accounts of the campaign agree regarding the great devastation wrought by Sherman's soldiers and their remarkable high spirits.

Melville had available a variety of such sources, but he certainly borrowed from *The Story of the Great March* (1865) by Major George Ward Nichols, a very popular book of which he owned a copy. The detail of the gamecocks and their names in stanza five, for example, seems to come from Major Nichols. The metaphor of the army as a river pouring down to the sea is all too obvious and it recurs in "The Muster," which describes the victorious troops, Sherman's among them, passing in review.

"The March to the Sea" was first published in *Harper's New Monthly Magazine* for February 1866. Melville revised two lines in the last stanza to express a milder attitude toward the South when he prepared the poem for publication in *Battle-Pieces*, and although there was little hope of a second edition, his personal copy shows further changes in the same direction.

A CANTICLE   [page 40]

The phrase "congregated Fall" in the second line of this hymn to victory is richly textured. It expands into the principal trope of the poem, a tremendous cataract surging over a precipice into a pool below and, as it swirls downward, forming white billows and a dazzling rainbow. It also calls to mind the Fall of Man and the fallen angels of the War in Heaven through subsequent lines in this poem and others in *Battle-Pieces* reminiscent of Milton's *Paradise Lost*. The fall of Richmond, which Melville credited with providing the original "impulse" for a volume of verses on the Civil War and is the subject of one of them (not presented here), is further suggested.

The imagery is so decidedly visual that it raises the question of whether Melville had in mind Niagara Falls, which he probably visited in 1840, or one of the many paintings he very likely saw on exhibition in New York, such as "The Great Fall, Niagara" by Frederick Edwin Church or "Sunrise at Niagara" by De Witt Clinton Boutelle.

Two important concepts are woven into the fabric of the poem: that of beauty and stability which exists, like the rainbow, transcendently and without a base; and that of the necessity to be ever aware of "The Giant of the Pool," an abiding threat to Iris, goddess of the rainbow. The reference to the woolly whiteness of the giant's forehead recalls the biblical visions of Daniel and, with other images of whiteness, the whale Moby-Dick, and the awful whiteness of the sea in Poe's *Narrative of Arthur Gordon Pym, of Nantucket,* which Melville had in his library.

THE MARTYR   [page 42]

John Wilkes Booth shot President Lincoln on Good Friday, April 14, 1865. The ironies of the time of his death did not escape Melville who, in identifying Lincoln as the redeemer and forgiver, further associates him with Christ, and hints that the "clemency and calm" of Lincoln's plans for political reconstruction will be more difficult than ever to implement. The emphasis on public grief and shock, with its consequent demand for revenge, is an ironical distortion of the meaning of Christ's sacrificial death and a method of stating the harsh realities that stand in the way of a policy of forgiveness toward the South. Melville supplied the following note on "The Avenger" in the second stanza:

At this period of excitement the thought was by some passionately welcomed that the Presidential successor had been raised up by heaven to wreak vengeance on the South. The idea originated in the remembrance that Andrew Johnson by birth belonged to that class of Southern whites who never cherished love for the dominant one; that he was a citizen of Tennessee, where the contest at times and in places had been close and bitter as a Middle-Age feud; that himself and family had been hardly treated by the Secessionists.

But the expectations built hereon (if, indeed, ever soberly entertained), happily for the country, have not been verified.

Likewise the feeling which would have held the entire South chargeable with the crime of one exceptional assassin, this too has died away with the natural excitement of the hour.

Melville asserts Lincoln's role as the father of his country, heightening the horror of assassination by depicting it as parricide. Lincoln was popularly called "Father Abraham," and biblically the name means "a father of many nations."

Yet the poem is not so much concerned with Lincoln the individual or with "the people" who respond to his death as with primordial forces which the event unleashed. The form of the poem, which suggests at first a traditional ballad and later a funeral chorus, is suitable to such a powerful but impersonal expression.

"THE COMING STORM"   [page 44]

Melville saw the painting, "The Coming Storm" by San-
ford R. Gifford, at the fortieth annual exhibition of the Na-
tional Academy of Design in New York. The owner, according
to the catalogue, was Edwin Booth, famous for his inter-
pretations of Shakespearean tragedy, particularly *Hamlet*,
and the brother of John Wilkes Booth, the actor who as-
sassinated Lincoln. When Edwin Booth learned of the circum-
stances of Lincoln's death, he retired temporarily from the
stage.

The subject of the landscape was not an unusual one at
the time, and Melville's references to it in the second stanza
are accurate enough. Apparently he attended the exhibition
just after Lincoln's death, in which case he would have noted
the association with Edwin Booth and with *Hamlet*. In *Bat-
tle-Pieces*, as here, "The Coming Storm" immediately follows
"The Martyr." Symbolically it represents the oppositions of
peace and war, and any "demon-cloud" that invades an
"urned lake." Melville concludes that such horrors are no
surprise to those who, like Edwin Booth, have reached the
core of Shakespeare's tragic vision.

REBEL COLOR-BEARERS AT SHILOH   [page 45]

The incident on which this piece is based is narrated
in a newspaper account of the battle to be found in the
"Rebellion Record." During the disaster to the national
forces on the first day, a brigade on the extreme left found
itself isolated. The perils it encountered are given in de-
tail. Among others, the following sentences occur:

"Under cover of the fire from the bluffs, the rebels
rushed down, crossed the ford, and in a moment were
seen forming this side of the creek in open fields, and
within close musket-range. Their color-bearers stepped de-
fiantly to the front as the engagement opened furiously;
the rebels pouring in sharp, quick volleys of musketry,

and their batteries above continuing to support them with a destructive fire. Our sharpshooters wanted to pick off the audacious rebel color-bearers, but Colonel Stuart interposed: 'No, no, they're too brave fellows to be killed.'"

(*Melville's Note*)

The quotation is transcribed by Melville with a single trivial change from an account originally published in the Cincinnati *Gazette* of April 9, 1862, and reprinted in *The Rebellion Record* (IV, 391). Through this note Melville reveals his indebtedness to *The Rebellion Record* as a source for *Battle-Pieces*.

THE MUSTER   [page 47]

According to a report of the Secretary of War, there were on the first day of March, 1865, 965,000 men on the army pay-rolls. Of these, some 200,000—artillery, cavalry, and infantry—made up from the larger portion of the veterans of Grant and Sherman, marched by the President. The total number of Union troops enlisted during the war was 2,668,000.

(*Melville's Note*)

The review before the President, army commanders, and other dignitaries took place in Washington on May 22–23, 1865.

Although Melville had Lincoln in mind when he used the epithet "Abrahamic" and had also compared an army to a river in "The March to the Sea," a discarded passage from his novel, *The Confidence-Man*, is pertinent: "As the word Abraham means father of a great multitude of men so the word Mississippi means father of a great multitude of waters. His tribes stream in from east and west. . . ." The river metaphor frames the poem, but internally the connections are subtly associational; e.g., "hazy" leads to "nebulously" which links to "Milky Way" and the stars in the flags borne by the soldiers.

"FORMERLY A SLAVE"   [page 48]

"Jane Jackson, formerly a Slave—Drawing in oil-color" by Elihu Vedder is listed in the 1865 exhibition catalogue of the National Academy of Design. Vedder used as a model "an old negro woman" whose "look of patient endurance" had impressed him. Melville felt the "prophetic" power of her countenance, a curious matter since Vedder later used the drawing as the basis of his more ambitious "Cumaean Sibyl."

In presenting the possibility that time will deal more kindly with her grandchildren than it had with Jane Jackson herself, Melville is consistent with his view of the healing quality of Nature operating over an extended period of history.

THE APPARITION   [page 49]

As in "The Coming Storm," a horror intrudes upon an idyllic, pastoral landscape. The "core," a crucial word in both poems, is of volcanic fire which forces its way through the seeming solidity of the earth's green crust.

The poem moves inductively, the first two stanzas furnishing the concrete example from which a logical conclusion is derived.

In *Mardi* (Chapter 122) Melville ends his exposition of the "Plutonian" geological origin of certain islands: "Thus Nature works, at random warring, chaos a crater, and the world a shell."

ON THE SLAIN COLLEGIANS   [page 50]

The records of Northern colleges attest what numbers of our noblest youth went from them to the battle-field. Southern members of the same class arrayed themselves on the side of Secession; while Southern seminaries contributed large quotas. Of all these, what numbers marched who never returned except on the shield.

(*Melville's Note*)

Having described the bitter battles and their implications and having celebrated the victory, Melville turns in the final war poems toward memorializing the dead in a manner that provides a basis for reconciliation. The slain collegians of both sides were honorable, valiant, loyal, and at one with each other in death. The poem harks back to the young soldiers of "The March into Virginia" and "Ball's Bluff" but with this difference: the collegians retain their innocence, like the first flowers of spring, which a chance storm kills "in their flush of bloom."

Educated in the classical tradition, the collegians had lived in a time like the golden age of Saturn and in surroundings that recalled the beautiful vale of Tempe at the base of Mount Olympus. It was to be expected that they would seek to emulate Apollo and "Each would slay his Python." Melville owned a reproduction of J. M. W. Turner's engraving "Apollo Killing the Python," extracted from the *Art Journal* (1860).

AMERICA [page 52]

This poem concludes the main section of *Battle-Pieces* and is followed in the first edition by a separation page and the "Verse Inscriptive and Memorial." As the concluding poem, it summarizes important themes and motifs, and it emphasizes brotherhood and reconciliation. The "sunny Dome" recalls the "Iron Dome" of the Capitol from "The Conflict of Convictions," and the reference to "Berenice's Hair," the constellation named for an Egyptian queen who pledged her locks to Venus to assure the safe return of her husband from war, is related to the "streaming beard" of John Brown, which is compared to a meteor in "The Portent."

In the first stanza, the starry banner of the statuesque young goddess, America, floats over the peaceful land where her children play. In the second it becomes a battle streamer as she watches the furious conflict of her children, and in the third it is a shroud for a deathlike sleep during which she has a vision of the horrors that lie at the "earth's foundation bare"—a phrase repeated from "The Conflict of Convictions." In the last stanza, she awakens, matured by her experience and affirmed in her adherence to "Law," able to face the future with calm assurance.

Melville had seen allegorical statues of "America" by Thomas Crawford and Hiram Powers.

ON THE HOME GUARDS [page 54]

In the group of memorial verses as in the *Battle-Pieces* proper, Melville followed a chronological arrangement. "On the Home Guards" is the initial poem of this section.

An outnumbered Union force under Colonel James A. Mulligan surrendered Lexington, Missouri, to General Sterling Price on September 20, 1861, after sporadic fighting that had begun eight days before. One reason for the Union defeat, contrary to what Melville suggests here, was the poor performance of the Home Guard.

THE FORTITUDE OF THE NORTH [page 54]

The Second Battle of Manassas took place on August 29–30, 1862, between the Confederate Army of Northern Virginia under General Lee and the Union Army of Virginia under General John Pope. The Confederate Army repeated its victory of July 21, 1861, fought on the same field.

For Melville, Cape Horn, the "Cape-of-Storms," was a place of great tribulation. He had rounded it as a seaman and a passenger, and in his journal of August 7, 1860, gave it this telling description: "Horrible snowy mountains—black, thunder-cloud woods—gorges—hell-landscapes."

INSCRIPTION   [page 55]

In his unsuccessful offensive against Lee's Army of Northern Virginia, General Ambrose E. Burnside, commanding the Union Army of the Potomac, crossed the Rappahannock River and fought his way through Fredericksburg, Virginia. On December 13, 1862, he faced Confederate troops under General James Longstreet entrenched behind a stone wall with a tight concentration of rifles and supporting artillery on the hill above. Some 12,700 Union soldiers were killed or wounded in repeated attempts to reach the wall.

Melville uses the word "erect" as his main verb, as a modifier of "Stone," and in contrast to "overthrown."

ON SHERMAN'S MEN   [page 55]

At Kennesaw Mountain near Marietta, Georgia, on June 26–27, 1864, Confederate General Joseph E. Johnston withstood fierce attacks by General William Tecumseh Sherman who was driving toward Atlanta. Johnston fell back when Sherman flanked his position.

ON THE GRAVE OF A YOUNG CAVALRY OFFICER   [page 56]

Through his delicate play on the words "Gold," "mind," "unenriched," and "fortune," Melville suggests that the young cavalry officer, so fortunate in his life, is even more fortunate in his death.

COMMEMORATIVE OF A NAVAL VICTORY [page 57]

Melville regarded highly the combination of strength and gentleness in such sailors as Jack Chase of the novel *White-*

Jacket and Billy Budd. They showed the tempering effect of naval discipline, "the wave," just as the fine steel swords of Damascus bear a distinctive wave or watered lines resulting from the way in which they are manufactured.

The Titian portrait may be "The Man with a Falcon." The "favored guest" may have been based upon Guert Gansevoort, Melville's first cousin, a naval officer of some distinction. His life had been darkened by his role as presiding officer of the court martial in 1842 that convicted Midshipman Philip Spencer and two sailors of mutiny in the controversial "Somers" case.

The proper renown earned by the naval hero carries with it a knowledge of the "light and shadow" in all things, including the motives and conduct of both sides in the Civil War. His "laurel wreath" mixed "with pensive pansies dark" should be compared to Timoleon's "laurel twined with thorn."

Sharks infest Melville's seas, notably in the poems "The Maldive Shark," "In a Bye-Canal," and "The Haglets."

A *Pilgrimage:* from CLAREL

On October 10, 1884, in reply to James Billson, an English admirer, Melville supplied details about the publication of several of his books. *Clarel* he described as "a metrical affair, a pilgrimage or what not . . . eminently adapted for unpopularity." This was the work which his wife Elizabeth had called in 1876 as it neared completion, a "dreadful *incubus*." Consisting of some 20,000 lines of verse divided into four parts and subdivided into 150 cantos, it was, like *Moby-Dick*, "a whale of a book." The magnitude of its scope, the intensity of the quest, the complexity of the probings, the range but pertinence of the digressions justify the comparison of *Clarel* with the great novel that had preceded it by a quarter of a century.

Clarel reflects Melville's own pilgrimage to Palestine in 1857. He landed at Jaffa on January 6, was in Jerusalem the following day, went on a tour of the Jordan Valley and Dead Sea, returned to Jerusalem, and sailed from Jaffa on January 24. Much of what went into his travel journal, fleshed out with subsequent reading, found its way into the poem. Melville had sought spiritual sustenance in the Holy Land but he did not find it, and he returned to examine his experience in his honest way, turning inward to discover the reason for his disappointment. The examination involved the nature of the times and the nature of the human soul. The results he called *Clarel: A Poem and Pilgrimage in the Holy Land.*

The poem as narrative and symbol is cast in the form of a quest. It focuses upon Clarel, a young American ministerial student whose pursuit of theology has raised irritating questions rather than brought spiritual peace. He meets Ruth, daughter of Nathan, an American farmer converted to Judaism and Zionism. They fall in love but Nathan is killed by Arab bandits and Ruth, according to a Jewish custom, is required to undergo a period of retirement. During this interval Clarel becomes one of a group of pilgrims who set out on a ten-day excursion that takes them to Jericho, the Jordan River, the Dead Sea and Siddim Plain, and the Monastery of Mar Saba in the mountains of Judah. Here they remain for three days and then depart for Bethlehem. They return to Jerusalem at sunrise on Ash Wednesday. In Clarel's absence Ruth has died of grief. His search for a resolution of faith and doubt ends inconclusively.

The characters who take part in the pilgrimage or are encountered in Jerusalem and along the way may have been first conceived to represent a particular point of view or a significant experience each had undergone, but Melville became enmeshed in their psychological complexities and they usually emerge as something more than vehicles for his ideas. The important characters in the order of their appearance here are: Celio, Rolfe, Nehemiah, Vine, Derwent, Mortmain, Margoth, and Ungar.

Celio, a hunchback with a handsome face, lives in a Franciscan monastery. His deformity has increased his bitterness, isolation, and doubts of the Roman Catholic faith.

Rolfe is both a thinker and a man of action. He is capable of enjoying the world while asking profound questions about it. His experiences as a sailor in the Pacific and his physical resemblance to Melville suggest the presence of autobiographical elements in this characterization.

Nehemiah is a devout though narrow sectarian whose religious views were originally shared by Clarel. In Jerusalem he had introduced Clarel to Ruth. His humility, charity, and unshakable faith make him a sympathetic though limited character.

Of the pilgrims, Vine, along with Rolfe, arouses the greatest response in Clarel. Vine is an American of middle age, possessed of unspecified creative talents and fine aesthetic and moral sensibilities. He is attractive but reserved. In the complex characterization of Vine, Melville seems to have been thinking of Hawthorne and to have had in mind their relationship.

Derwent, an Anglican churchman, is pleasant and gracious and stands for a religion which emphasizes these qualities. He believes in the goodness of man, the idea of progress, and the beneficence of Nature. Though personable, he is superficial. When the troubled Clarel turns to him as a mature, experienced priest, he can offer no help.

Mortmain, a tormented Swede, was once an idealistic revolutionary but has been disillusioned to such an extent that he can do little but rail at what strikes him as the evil in man and turn self-destructively upon himself. What hurts Mortmain most is his feeling that the inevitable result of the emulation of Christ on earth is crucifixion.

Margoth, born a Jew but rejecting his religion for a crude utilitarianism, is a geologist who delights in using his science to attack religious faith.

Ungar is a former officer in the Confederate Army, now a professional soldier in the pay of the Turks. His religious background is Roman Catholic, and his family has a strain of Indian blood. His life in the South during the Civil War and Reconstruction has made him skeptical of American political institutions. Convinced, like Mortmain, of man's fallen state, he feels the need for religion without adhering to any particular sect.

PART I, CANTO XIII, THE ARCH   [page 60]

Exploring the environs of Jerusalem with Nehemiah as his guide, Clarel visits Lower Gihon, one of two pools with biblical associations which are west of the city. Here he first encounters Celio. Although neither speaks, Celio senses in Clarel "A brother that he might own / In tie of spirit" and Clarel reacts with "A novel sympathy." Each had begun to question the validity of his religious beliefs.

Line 10
Immediately before Clarel saw Celio, he had come upon "three demoniacs" whom he identified with the Gadarene man possessed by devils (Luke 8:27). Here, Melville implies that Clarel and Celio were likewise bedeviled.

Line 20
The Via Crucis or Via Dolorosa is the road traversed by Christ from the palace of Pontius Pilate to the place of Crucifixion.

Lines 22–27

In his travel journal under the heading "Interior of Jerusalem" Melville wrote: "The arch—the stone he leaned against —the stone of Lazarus &c. City like a quarry—all stone. —Vaulted ways—buttresses (flying) Arch (*Ecce Homo*)." The Ecce Homo Arch spans the Via Dolorosa and is said to be the place where Pilate presented Christ to the populace for judgment.

Line 36

Cf. Pilate's words to the mob, "Behold your King!" (John 19:14).

Line 47

Cf. the words of Christ on the Cross, "My God, my God, why hast thou forsaken me?" (Mark 15:34).

Line 74

"Then came the Jews round about him, and said unto him, How long dost thou make us to doubt? If thou be the Christ, tell us plainly." (John 10:24).

Line 95

The face of Medusa, the snake-haired monster whose countenance turned men to stone, adorned the shield carried by Athene.

Line 104

Celio's disorientation during his wanderings reflects his loss of spiritual direction.

Lines 110–18

Celio identifies himself with the legendary Wandering Jew, doomed to travel the earth until Judgment Day for having taunted Christ as he bore the Cross to Calvary. At the Monastery of Mar Saba the pilgrims see a religious masque on the subject of the Wandering Jew.

PART I, CANTO XXXVII, A SKETCH   [page 64]

From the tower of the church on the summit of the Mount
of Olives, the pilgrims have viewed for the first time the
Judah Wilderness and, in the distance, the Dead Sea. They
have been deeply impressed, all except the meek, unworldly
Nehemiah who proposes a "Fair stroll" to nearby Bethany
which he calls "a pleasant town." His suggestion is out of keep-
ing with the mood induced by what the pilgrims have seen
from the tower. They are puzzled by his failure to be touched
as they have been, and do not accept his proposal.

Line 31
Calvin, with his emphasis on predestination, and Zeno,
the Greek stoic philosopher, are Christian and classical re-
sponses to Fate which are rejected by the captain in Rolfe's
story.

Lines 38–105
On November 20, 1820, while on a whaling cruise of the
Pacific, the *Essex*, commanded by Captain George Pollard,
Jr., of Nantucket, was sunk by the head-on blows from a
whale. Fearful of cannibals on nearby islands, the crew of
twenty set out in three whaleboats for the two-thousand-mile
voyage to the coast of South America. After terrible priva-
tions and the resort to cannibalism, eight men survived, in-
cluding Pollard and his first mate, Owen Chase. Pollard went
to sea again as captain of another whaler but lost his ship on
a reef. He never obtained another command and became a
night watchman at Nantucket where he died in 1870. Chase
was more fortunate, twice returning from successful whaling
cruises. However, he is said to have had marital difficulties
and in his old age to have hidden supplies of food about the
house.

Melville mentions Pollard in *Moby-Dick* (Chapter 45)
and looked upon the destruction of the *Essex* by a sperm
whale as corroborative evidence for the sinking of the *Pequod*
in this novel. He met William Chase, son of Owen Chase,

in the South Pacific in 1841 and "questioned him concerning his father's adventure"; he first read Chase's *Narrative of the Extraordinary and Distressing Shipwreck of the Whale-Ship Essex* (1821) at that time; and he was given a copy by Lemuel Shaw, his father-in-law, in April 1851. On July 8, 1852, Melville visited Nantucket and met Pollard. In his copy of Chase's *Narrative*, he described him in an annotation as "the most impressive man, tho' wholly unassuming, even humble—that I ever encountered."

Line 106
An Italian dramatist, Sylvio Pellico was imprisoned by the Austrians for revolutionary activities in the early 1820s. His most memorable work is an account of his imprisonment, *Le Mie prigióni* (1832). In Melville's poem "Pausilippo," not reprinted here, Pellico's misfortunes are said to have rendered him "spiritless and spent."

Line 116
In his lecture, "Statues in Rome," Melville refers to the Laocoön group in the Vatican. A priest of Apollo, Laocoön and his two sons were crushed by serpents from the sea, perhaps as punishment for his profaning the temple or for having warned the Trojans against the wooden horse of the Greeks. In this lecture Melville described Laocoön as "a great and powerful man, writhing with the inevitable destiny he cannot throw off," who represented "the tragic side of humanity and is the symbol of human misfortune."

PART II, CANTO XXVII, VINE AND CLAREL
[page 68]

When the pilgrims reach the Jordan River, at Rolfe's suggestion they sing the medieval hymn, "Ave maris stella." Their voices attract a Dominican monk, a pious but sophisticated French Canadian. His presence leads to a discussion of Catholicism in the three cantos immediately preceding. A Greek banker and his future son-in-law—representatives of wealth and worldly pleasure, who had been members of the party that left Jerusalem—had turned back at the edge of the

Wilderness, leaving behind a supply of wine with which the pilgrims refresh themselves while they rest.

Line 11

The "Venetian slats" may be compared with the eyes "Between the slats" which attract and endanger in the poem "In a Bye-Canal."

Lines 17–21

Melville had visited the Cathedral, Baptistery, and Leaning Tower of Pisa on March 23, 1857. "Clarel leaned" in the pursuit of his self-destructive hunger for "communion true" (l. 69) with Vine. The phrase recalls Melville's poem, "Pisa's Leaning Tower," which "thinks to plunge—but hesitates; / Shrinks back—yet fain would slide; / . . . A would-be suicide."

Line 87

Sir Philip Sidney, the English poet, statesman, and soldier, received a mortal wound at Zutphen in 1586. He is reputed to have refused a cup of water so that it might be given to a dying soldier, saying "Thy necessity is yet greater than mine."

Lines 113–32

Vine's withdrawal when he senses the implications of Clarel's overtures suggests not only the difficulty of the kind of intimacy that Clarel yearns for (cf. "Monody") but its inadequacy for souls "tried by doubt." Clarel's doubt and his temptation to avoid the lonely search by merging himself in brotherhood with Vine is contrasted with Nehemiah's solitary beatitude (ll. 145–66).

PART II, CANTO XXXI, THE INSCRIPTION
[page 73]

On the third day the travelers reach the Siddim Plain along the northern margin of the Dead Sea. They pause while Rolfe describes the ruins of the fortress city of Petra, hidden from view by awesome mountains. The hellish landscape is appalling, although Nehemiah naps peacefully in the shade of the rock bearing the "Slanting Cross" and inscription.

Lines 29–40
Rolfe compares the chalked design to the constellation, the Southern Cross. His point is that the constellation is not stable but becomes progressively colder and more remote. The verse inscription (ll. 53–73) amplifies this idea.

Lines 53–59
A similar reference to the reduction of the ancient gods to heraldic emblems occurs in the second stanza of "The Temeraire."

Lines 69–71
When Orion, the giant hunter, was accidentally killed by Artemis, she transformed him into one of the most spectacular constellations. The center of this constellation also forms a cross.

PART II, CANTO XXXIV, MORTMAIN REAPPEARS
[page 76]

After camping for the night beside the Dead Sea, the pilgrims explore its shore and hear Margoth disparage the biblical account of its origin until the braying of a donkey puts an end to his geological explanations. The absence of Mortmain, who had chosen to remain behind for a day or two at Elisha's Fountain near the wilderness where Christ was tempted by Satan, has caused uneasiness.

Line 10
Hekla is a volcano seventy miles east of Reykjavik, Iceland. It had last erupted in 1845. Melville refers to Hekla humorously in *Moby-Dick* (Chapter 3) and to its deceptive appearance in the poem, "The Battle for the Bay," not reprinted here.

Line 20
Cherith is a brook in the Jordan Valley where Elijah took

refuge. After it dried up, Elijah was told by God to begin his prophecy (I Kings 17).

Lines 30–38

The topical references in Mortmain's call to repentance may be to the end of the Franco-Prussian War (ll. 33–34) and the Paris Commune (ll. 37–38). Mortmain had once been a rebel and free thinker.

Lines 39–40

Rolfe sees Mortmain as a secular John the Baptist, another voice "crying in the wilderness" for repentance (Matthew 3:1–3).

Line 63

In the wilderness of Shûr, the Israelites, after three days without water, found the bitter wells of Marah (Exodus 15:22–23).

Line 65

The name Mortmain means the hand of death and suggests the impulse toward self-destruction.

PART II, CANTO XXXV, PRELUSIVE   [page 78]

Melville's reflections on the prints in the sequence "Imaginary Prisons," of Giovanni Battista Piranesi follow Mortmain's drink from the Dead Sea and are prelusive to his discussion of the depravities ("not all carnal harlotry, / But sins refined, crimes of the spirit") which brought about the destruction of Sodom. Piranesi's set of sixteen etchings was executed in the 1740s when he was about twenty-five. Highly romantic and theatrical, they captivated Coleridge and his description of them, as recorded in De Quincey's *Confessions of an English Opium Eater* (1822), is close in language and spirit to Melville's. In the Victorian period, however, interest in Piranesi declined severely. Ruskin ignores him, but Melville found in the "Imaginary Prisons" a visual expression of the "mystery of iniquity" which so intrigued him.

Line 12

Rhadamanthus was one of the judges of the dead in Hades, an office he held because of his absolute integrity.

Line 24

This Pauline phrase (II Thessalonians 2:7) recurs in *Billy Budd* and elsewhere.

PART III, CANTO XXXII, EMPTY STIRRUPS
[page 80]

From the Dead Sea the travelers proceed through the wilderness and up the mountains of Judah to the Monastery of Mar Saba. Here they rest, drink the famous local wine, wander about the fifth-century convent, watch the monks at their rituals, and observe a palm tree high on a ledge above, seemingly a token of the promise of grace. After three days at Mar Saba, and on the seventh day of their pilgrimage, they assemble at dawn to depart for Bethlehem nine miles away. Mortmain does not appear.

Lines 15–16

The reference is to the reception of the prophet Elijah by the devout governor, Obadiah, in I Kings 18.

Line 22

An entry in Melville's travel journal under the heading "From Jerusalem to Dead Sea &c." describes his visit to Mar Saba, a great tourist attraction. The monastery consists of a series of terraces built against the almost vertical wall of a gorge. Melville noted "numerous terraces, *balconies—solitary Date Palm mid-way in precipice—*." The palm was said to have been planted by St. Saba. It is an important symbol in Part III. Derwent, Vine, Mortmain, Rolfe, and Clarel all respond to it variously but in ways suitable to the particular nature of each. Technically, Melville's use of the palm recalls the response of the members of the crew in *Moby-Dick* (Chapter 99) as, one by one, they scrutinized the doubloon that Captain Ahab nailed to the mast.

PART IV, CANTO XXI, UNGAR AND ROLFE
[page 83]

The austere professional soldier, Ungar, joins the pilgrims as they depart from Mar Saba. Reticent at first, he is soon revealed as an outspoken critic of society and human nature. He disturbs the equable Derwent with his discussion of religion but finds a sympathetic audience for his observations on democracy, reform, and the prospects for the New World in Don Hannibal, a convivial Mexican patriot who has also joined the party. Rolfe senses the suffering that has brought such bitter wisdom to Ungar and encourages him to talk.

Lines 32–39
Cf. Job 21:1–15 on the wicked who, in their prosperity, ask, "What is the Almighty, that we should serve him? and what profit should we have, if we pray unto him?"

Lines 38–39
Cf. Joshua 10:12–13 where it is recorded that in the valley of Ajalon "the sun stood still, and the moon stayed until the people had avenged themselves upon their enemies."

PART IV, CANTO XXII, OF WICKEDNESS THE WORD [page 88]

Ungar's grim observations, deeply affecting his hearers, reach their climax as he shifts his attention from the future of America to the basis of all of his assumptions—the evil in the hearts of men and the necessity for regeneration.

Lines 24–29
Ungar's complaint that the original meaning of "wickedness the word" has been lost parallels references to the decline of faith into myth and of meaningful symbols into mere ornament of which Mortmain's verses on the "Slanting Cross" in "The Inscription" is one example. Melville demonstrates a grasp of philology as well as theology. Ungar's discussion is reminiscent of Mortmain's speculations on the

nature of the sins that caused Sodom to be sunk beneath the waters of the Dead Sea. See the comment on "Prelusive," p. 206.

Line 43

Ungar, though religious, is not narrowly sectarian but neither is he like Derwent so broad and bland as to seem without a rooted faith. He argues for spiritual rebirth, echoing Christ's words in John 3:7, "Ye must be born again."

Lines 59–61

Together Derwent and Clarel had watched the sunrise from the tower of Mar Saba. Because of his natural kindliness, and in his office of priest seeking to help a theological student in spiritual distress, Derwent encouraged Clarel to speak freely and at the same time revealed without reserve his own spiritual state. Clarel was repelled by the thinness of Derwent's faith while Derwent could only reply, "Alas, too deep you dive."

PART IV, CANTO XXXIV, VIA CRUCIS [page 91]

The travelers spend three days in Bethlehem and depart on the ninth night of their pilgrimage for Jerusalem, arriving at the outskirts of the city at dawn on Ash Wednesday. Clarel, who has had forebodings about Ruth, sees gravediggers at work. Ruth and her mother have died of fever and grief. For Clarel the period of Lent is one of wracking anguish and doubt, intensified by the experience of his pilgrimage and the death of his betrothed. By Good Friday his fellow pilgrims have left and his memories of Celio, Nehemiah, Mortmain, Ruth, and others now dead who had touched his heart, enhance his misery. Even the Easter celebration, the subject of the Canto immediately preceding, leaves him unmoved, though the Canto concludes, "Sluggish, life's wonted stream flows on." The flow of life along paths which seem to follow the line of least resistance is the subject of the opening stanza of "Via Crucis."

Line 19

In the comments on Jerusalem in his travel journal, Melville wrote: "*Thoughts in the Via Dolorosa*—women panting under burdens—men with melancholy faces." His recollection of what he had seen along the road from St. Stephen's Gate to the Church of the Holy Sepulcher, the traditional route of Christ bearing the Cross, underlies this Canto and especially the important reference to "Cross-bearers all" (l. 43) which holds forth a possibility of consolation through an awareness of the brotherhood in passion of all living creatures.

Line 22

Whitsunday or Pentecost is the fiftieth day after Easter, the third of the major Christian holy days, and the last in the annual cycle that celebrates the life of Christ. It commemorates the descent of the Holy Spirit upon the apostles in the form of "cloven tongues like as of fire" (Acts 2:1–4).

Line 49

See "Pebbles" (III) for "liquid hills" which have no echo.

Line 51

The allusion is to the Atlantic Cable, then an exciting advance in communications.

PART IV, CANTO XXXV, EPILOGUE   [page 93]

In the "Epilogue" the poet speaks directly to Clarel who is last seen vanishing into silence and darkness. Yet the direction of both the poem and its protagonist has been toward consolation. A thread from the previous Canto, the allusion to Whitsunday, is picked up and developed significantly. Whitsunday, one of the principal occasions for baptism, derives its name from the white garments worn by those participating in this rite. This allusion appears to be linked with a baptism in "the last whelming sea" (l. 33). Melville has other such baptisms in the sea, notably at the end of *Moby-Dick* where Ishmael survives the sinking of the *Pequod* and at the climax of *White-Jacket* when the young sailor is rescued after having fallen from the mainmast into the sea. Cf. also the healing through the agency of the "inhuman Sea" in "Pebbles" (VII).

Sailors and the Sea

JOHN MARR   [page 96]

Not only is "John Marr" the initial poem but it is also a prologue, establishing point of view and tone, to the little book that Melville called *John Marr and Other Sailors with Some Sea-Pieces* (1888). The prose sketch introduces a landlocked old seaman, cast ashore among simple farmers who are pioneering the vast, oceanic prairie. Though the fault lies beyond anyone's control, there is no bond of affection or even understanding between the sailor and people so different from himself. Therefore he turns inward and backward to memories of his shipmates and the past which they shared. At this point the prose preface merges into the poem.

The use of a prose preface which all but overwhelms the verse that follows it seems to be in part an attempt to evolve a new literary form and in part an outgrowth of Melville's tendency to expand and expatiate upon his germinal material. Among Melville's posthumously published writings are two such examples of combined prose and verse, "Rammon" and "Rip Van Winkle's Lilac." He attempted considerably less but achieved better balance with "Tom Deadlight" where his preface is a bare headnote. Recent textual scholarship indicates that Melville's novella, *Billy Budd*, evolved from the poem, "Billy in the Darbies," with which it terminates.

It is difficult to divorce Melville himself from his spokesman. Certainly poems like "Tom Deadlight" and "Jack Roy" emerge from the texture of his own life as a sailor a full generation before he published his nostalgic, cathartic "sea-pieces" and verses about seamen.

TOM DEADLIGHT   [page 104]

A deadlight is a thick pane of glass set in the deck of a ship to provide illumination below. Thus Melville has given his old petty officer a name suitable to his occupation and to his condition, a name that he delicately exploits throughout the poem. The sailor is himself a dying light but the manner of his death can make him a source of enlightenment (cf. "enlightened" in "The March into Virginia") to those left groping in the darkness. The name also clarifies his seemingly confused ramblings, what Melville calls in the headnote the "last flutterings of distempered thought."

As the sight of the dying man begins to fail, the ship seems to be encountering navigational difficulties. There is a "black scud a' flying" and "the light-ship is hid by the mist." Neither pilotage nor celestial navigation is possible under such circumstances, but "Dead reckoning" remains available and is the proper means when heading "for the Deadman," despite the advice of "Joe." "The Deadman" is Dodman's Point, a landmark near Plymouth, England. "Joe" is the ship's chaplain, "Holy Joe." And the "Lord High Admiral" who is watching "the grand fleet," another name for the British Channel Fleet, will someday order the last reckoning and review for all his sailors. So much for the tough old petty officer's final, unsentimental testament.

The "famous old sea-ditty" which forms the substructure of the poem is the ballad, "Farewell to You, Ye Fine Spanish Ladies." In *Moby-Dick* (Chapter 40) sailors and harpooners sing "Spanish Ladies" at midnight in the forecastle, and in *White-Jacket* (Chapter 74) it is sung by the handsome English sailor, Jack Chase, and called "a favourite thing with British man-of-war's men." A widely known version begins:

Now farewell to you, ye fine Spanish ladies;
Now farewell to you, ye ladies of Spain!
For we've received orders to sail for old England,
And perhaps we may never more see you again.

It contains references to "the Deadman," orders "for the grand fleet to anchor," instructions to "clear your shank painters," and a proposal for a final toast.

JACK ROY   [page 106]

As Melville states in the preface to *White-Jacket*, in "the year 1843, the author shipped as a common sailor on board of a United States frigate in a harbour in the Pacific Ocean. After serving on board of this frigate for more than a year, he was discharged, with the rest of the crew, upon the vessel's arrival home." His shipmates included Jack Chase, captain of the maintop, to Melville an ideal example of manliness and a blend of the best attributes of the gentleman and the commoner. He is one of the major figures in *White-Jacket*, and Melville dedicated his last book, *Billy Budd*, to him. In "Jack Roy" Melville once more recalls Jack Chase and episodes connected with him, this time with the particular purpose of affirming, in the face of human mortality, the enduring nature of what Chase represented. Therefore Jack Roy, unlike the sailors who once sang at the halyards but have since "Dropped mute," does not die (cf. Billy Budd and the admiral in "The Haglets") but rises from "a thousand fathoms down" with a love song on his lips.

Allusions to singing envelop the poem, from the "blithe chorus" at the beginning to the "Larking" at the end, the latter word implying playfulness as well as birdlike song (cf. "larks ashore," last line of first stanza of "John Marr"). The sportive tone of the poem is re-enforced by the references to Mercutio, the gentleman wit and punster in Shakespeare's *Romeo and Juliet*, and by punning on the name, "Jack Roy," which in association with "king" and "knave" suggests the gamesomeness of card players. Cf. the "gallant off-handed" Mad Jack in *White-Jacket* (Chapter 85).

THE HAGLETS   [page 107]

According to Melville's travel journal, on December 7, 1856, while his ship was anchored in the harbor of Salonica, the "Captain told a story about the heat of arms affecting the compass." The next day, among the miscellaneous jottings in his journal, Melville wrote the sentence, "Arms taken

down into cabin after being discharged," and the marginal
note above, "*Cap. T's Story of arms.*" This is the germ of
"The Haglets" and "The Timoneer's Story" in *Clarel* (III,
xii, 57–130, not included here). It also recalls the epi-
sode in *Moby-Dick* (Chapter 124), published five years ear-
lier in 1851, of Captain Ahab's use of the steel of a whaling
lance to correct a compass that had been inverted by light-
ning. The timoneer or pilot in *Clarel* tells how his ship was
wrecked in a gale because the compass had been affected by
a box of swords hidden in a cabin beneath it. His story also
shares with "The Haglets" ominous corposants and sea birds:

> Corposants on yard-arms did burn,
> Red lightning forked upon the stern:
> The needle like an imp did spin.
> Three gulls continual plied in wake, . . .

The earliest version of "The Haglets" is the poem, "The
Admiral of the White," a title that comes from the white
ensign with the red cross of St. George in the upper left cor-
ner flown by the admiral commanding the squadron in the
van of the formation. "The Admiral of the White" was ap-
parently written about 1860 but not published until after
Melville's death. It consists of sixty-two lines in twelve stanzas
of from four to eight lines and presents essentially the same
incident as "The Haglets" but in quite different language
and with a conclusion that relatively is shallow. Except for
the incident, in no important respects are the poems com-
parable. What Melville seems to have been attempting was
a sea ballad in the tradition of "Sir Patrick Spens," from
which he had quoted in *White-Jacket* (Chapter 74).

On Sunday, May 17, 1885, the first published version of
"The Haglets," retaining the original title, appeared in the
New-York *Daily Tribune* and the Boston *Herald*. It is an
abridgment of "The Haglets" as it appears three years later
in *John Marr*, with the omissions indicated by ellipses. The
printer's copy for *John Marr*, in fact, consists of the *Tribune*
clipping cut apart and fitted in with the manuscript pages.

Melville's particularly careful instructions to the printer
about spacing and indentation show his concern with the

formal structure of the poem in its final version. This consists of three divisions: two six-line stanzas as a prologue or invocation to the spirit of the chapel by the sea; a main body of twelve eighteen-line stanzas; and an epilogue of three stanzas, the last two departing from the established metrical pattern. The main body of the poem is a modification of the *canzone*. Melville, who knew Spenser's poetry well (he owned the 1855 edition of Francis J. Child), had the example of his "Epithalamion" and "Prothalamion." His emulation of the *canzone* was ambitious and unusual for a poem of such length.

The prologue is a call for an explanation of the origin of the "memorial stone" and the significance of the emblems which adorn it—the effigy with "swords at feet, / Trophies at head, and kelp for a winding-sheet." The poem proper is a fairly straightforward account of the disaster that overtakes the flagship of the Admiral of the White as it speeds homeward with news of its victory and a cargo of Spanish loot. But the story itself raises more questions than it answers, the foremost being "Must victors drown— / Perish, even as the vanquished did?" And throughout the poem, the three haglets which had "followed late the flag-ship quelled," follow the British ship. The imagery of the last stanza of the main division sets forth their role unmistakably. They are the three Fates working at the loom of human destiny, spinning, weaving, and locking the web. The epilogue presents an answer and a reconciliation, at least in transcendent terms. It is ironic that at the moment just prior to enjoying the fruits of victory, man should be cast down. Yet this is within the tragic pattern, since man is flawed with pride, predacity, and heedlessness. The Admiral and his men die well, like Sir Patrick Spens and his sailors of the ballad:

> 'Tis fifty fathoms deep,
> And there lies gude Sir Patrick Spens,
> Wi' the Scots lords at his feet.

Death cleanses and leads to transformation, to a sea change as magical as that of Ariel's song of the drowned king in Shakespeare's *The Tempest* (I, ii, 396–403); and there is, furthermore, the intimation that the Admiral is not dead at all but deep in an "Unfathomable sleep," a condition foreshadowed by his being described as in "repose" and dozing "in drowsy light." In any event, the haglets cannot now penetrate his peaceful state. His sleep is like that of the transfigured sailor in the poem at the end of *Billy Budd* who is likewise "fathoms down" with seaweed twisted about him, living seaweed which in both poems hints Nature has prevailed over death.

The final stanza, though remote from the specific detail of the rest of the poem, reveals its significance and clarifies the basis of reconciliation. Trapped by time, man cannot see the unity of Nature that becomes apparent when single events are placed within a context outside of time. One man or one event is of little consequence to Nature, which exists beyond the moment and is without interest in the affairs of man. Stars shine and waves roll. Melville presents this idea, however, in spatial rather than temporal metaphor. The meteors high in the heavens "play," the waves on the surface of the sea "dance," and the Oreads or mountain nymphs and the elves "advance" to join them. The sky above and the depths of the sea merge in a unity of Nature's immutable processes.

A haglet or kittiwake is a small sea gull. An alternate spelling is "hacklet."

THE ÆOLIAN HARP   [page 114]

A musical instrument first described in the seventeenth century by Athanasius Kircher, the æolian harp is placed so that air passes obliquely across its strings causing them to vibrate. The name is derived from Æolus, god of the winds. In the opening quatrain Melville accurately depicts the shrill dissonances which soften into plaintive harmonies as the force of the wind subsides. The metaphor of the æolian harp was a favorite of the Romantic poets for whom it signified the role of the artist in the creative process and was important to the Transcendentalists as a representation of the phenomenon of inspiration. Melville owned an æolian harp. One owned by Emerson may be seen on display in his study at Concord.

Melville reviewed John Codman's *Sailor's Life and Sailor's Yarns* for the *Literary World* of March 6, 1847. In Codman's book is an account of a "dismasted and water-logged" derelict which "sluggishly rose and fell in the trough of the sea, wallowing like one of its huge monsters, dead" (pp. 74–75). In *Redburn* (Chapter 22), Melville has a similar floating wreck:

> It was a dismantled, water-logged schooner, a most dismal sight, that must have been drifting about for several long weeks. The bulwarks were pretty much gone; and here and there the bare *stanchions*, or posts, were left standing, splitting in two the waves which broke clear over the deck, lying almost even with the sea. The foremast was snapt off less than four feet from its base; and the shattered and splintered remnant looked like the stump of a pine tree in the woods. . . . everyone supposed her to be a New Brunswick lumberman.

In Shakespeare's *The Tempest* (I, ii) the spirit Ariel reports to Prospero on the harmless storm at sea the magician had ordered him to raise for purposes of deception. Hence "Ariel's rendering of the Real" belongs to the realm of fantasy or false reality, while true reality consists of a sea that is inhabited by derelicts, icebergs (cf. "The Berg") and sharks (cf. "The Maldive Shark") drifting about with an aimless, dumb fatality.

FAR OFF-SHORE [page 116]

By capitalizing on the aural association of "Cries" and "Crew," Melville gives added meaning to the onomatopoeic call of the sea birds, and by juxtaposing masculine and feminine rhymes, he obtains increased emphasis on the rhymed words "dead" and "crew." Hovering birds which suggest the detachment of Nature and Fate often accompany the dead (cf. "Shiloh") and the doomed (cf. "The Haglets") in Melville's poetry.

THE TUFT OF KELP [page 116]

The "dripping" kelp is related to the "dripping trophy" of the quatrain, "In a Garret." Though the former is a mere weed cast up by the ocean and the latter is associated with sumptuous gems attainable only after great effort, both are touched by the dark knowledge and elemental vitality that lie within the depths of the sea.

THE MALDIVE SHARK [page 117]

Among the memorable and comparable sharks in Melville's novels are "the ghastly White Shark" of *Mardi* (Chapter 13), and the shark in *Moby-Dick* (Chapter 42) with its "white gliding ghostliness of repose." In the poem, "Commemorative of a Naval Victory," the shark "Glides white through the phosphorus sea" and in "In a Bye-Canal" the poet undergoes an initiation " 'Twixt the whale's black flukes and the white shark's fin." A parallel to the symbiotic relation of the shark and pilot fish occurs in a quotation from Montaigne's "Apology for Raimond Sebond" (*Essays*, Book II, Chapter 12) appearing as one of the prefatory "Extracts" to *Moby-Dick*:

And whereas all the other things, whether beast or vessel, that enter into the dreadful gulf, are immediately lost and swallowed up, the sea-gudgeon retires into it in great security, and there sleeps.

The passage immediately preceding, which Melville does not quote, tells how the sea-gudgeon serves as a "guide" to the whale, and that which follows has other examples of such "partnerships." Comparison should also be made with Chapter 18 of *Mardi*, entitled "My Lord Shark and his Pages," which begins:

There is a fish in the sea that ever more like a surly lord, only goes abroad when attended by his suite. It is the Shovel-nosed Shark. A clumsy, lethargic monster, unshapely as his name, and the last species of his kind, one would think, to be so bravely waited upon as he is. His suite is composed of those dainty little creatures called Pilot fish by sailors.

In the poem Melville is considering the coexistence, even interdependence, of good and evil; the sharing of innocence and guilt; and the nature of devouring Fate, itself lethargic but well served by energy. A related but more affirmative application of the same metaphor appears in *Pierre* (Book IV, Chapter 2): "As the vine flourishes, and the grape empurples close up to the very walls and muzzles of cannoned Ehrenbreitstein; so do the sweetest joys of life grow in the very jaws of its perils" (cf. "when peril's abroad, / An asylum in jaws of the Fates!").

The Maldive Islands are an archipelago of coral atolls in the Indian Ocean some 400 miles southwest of Ceylon. The mythological Gorgons were three sisters with snakes for hair, so hideous that merely to look upon them turned men to stone. In *Mardi* (Chapter 18) Melville also associates sharks with the Gorgons.

THE BERG   [page 118]

The destruction of the ship which sails so willfully into the iceberg is another expression of Melville's sense of the limitations inherent in the universe. The ship may be handsomely appointed and commanded with energy and skill, but in its defiance of the primordial forces which the iceberg signifies it is "infatuate." The iceberg, however, is likewise compounded of attractive features—such as its delicate crystal tracery—and repellent qualities—such as its aimlessness and lumpishness. While emphasis is on the ship that, "Directed as by madness," destroys itself, it should be noted that the iceberg is also doomed, "dissolving, bound for death." In this pessimistic statement, therefore, Melville does not merely assert human limitations, though they are clearly greater than those placed upon objects of Nature like the iceberg, but the limitations applicable to natural objects as well. Note the important repetition of the word "down."

In his personal copy Melville cancelled the words in the last line, "dead indifference," and substituted "dense stolidity," echoing the initial description of the iceberg in the fourth line and underscoring its essential unconcern.

THE ENVIABLE ISLES   [page 120]

Evidence from Melville's manuscripts indicates that "The Enviable Isles" antedates the uncompleted "Rammon," was incorporated into this experimental combination of prose and verse, and was later removed and published separately in *John Marr*. In "Rammon" a contemplative, despondent prince, the son of Solomon, who feels that "cessation of being was the desirable event," seeks information on Oriental thought regarding immortality from Zardi, a widely traveled Tyrian trader. He addresses Zardi in the concluding lines of the verse section of the fragment:

> Fable me, then, those Enviable Isles
> Whereof King Hiram's tars used to tell;
> Now looms the dim shore when the land is ahead;
> And what the strange charm the tarrier beguiles
> Time without end content there to dwell.
> Ay, fable me, do, those enviable isles.

"The Enviable Isles" recalls Melville's more attractive portrayals of Polynesia, and "The Tahiti Islands," a title found among the "Rammon" manuscripts, may be an alternate one for this poem. In "To Ned," a nostalgic poem about "Authentic Edens in a Pagan sea," included in *John Marr* but not reprinted here, Melville speculates on a heavenly paradise: "Marvelling mild if mortal twice, / Here and hereafter, touch a Paradise." "The Enviable Isles" are the Isles of the Dead, where sleep is synonymous with death ("die," the last word of the final line is used in this double sense) and where at long last there is some kind of refuge from the storm. But to the extent that any paradise, earthly or heavenly, is comprised of sleep, it is a decidedly limited one. Other notable poems on the themes of indolence, sleep, passivity, and negativism are "The Bench of Boors" and "Buddha." It should be remembered that Tommo in *Typee* seeks to escape from the South Sea island paradise partly because "the greater business of life" for the natives is sleep (Chapter 20). A similar situation occurs in *Mardi* where the seekers, after a severe storm (cf. opening line), find a haven in Serenia. On this island brotherhood prevails, a realistic view of mankind's limitations is taken, and the human condition is considerably above the vegetable state of Typee. Even so the principal quester, Taji, continues his voyage, though his companion, the philosopher Babbalanja, is content to remain.

It would seem that "The Enviable Isles" is in the same vein as Tennyson's "The Lotos-Eaters," James Thomson's *Castle of Indolence,* and Spenser's *Faerie Queene* (I, i, 36–42). Melville owned the works of these poets.

PEBBLES [page 121]

The manuscript reveals that Melville considered calling this group of poems "Epigrams." The rejected title is appropriate, for the poems are a series of pointed statements summarizing various ideas present in *John Marr* and serving as its conclusion. Though more skillful and complex, "Pebbles," in its form, tone, and terminal position, may be compared with "Herba Santa," which separates the *Timoleon* poems from the subdivision of the same volume entitled "Fruit of Travel from Long Ago."

Like *John Marr* when considered as a whole, the seven parts of "Pebbles" consist of meaningful insights based upon objects and experiences which the sea has provided. In "Pebbles" they form a sequence. Part I affirms the superior wisdom of fish and seafowl that defer to the ways of the natural world in contrast to scientific, legalistic man who seeks to control Nature. Part II avers that unlike man's world of

shifting schools and creeds, the natural world, as represented
by the monotone heard when a conch shell is held to the ear,
never deviates or varies. Part III emphasizes the indifference
of the sea to the efforts, hopes, and dreams of man. Part IV
states that the sea is not just indifferent but permits man's
existence on sufferance only. Part V asserts the destructive
powers of the sea and the particular horror of the deceptive
calm that follows the storm. Part VI raises the question of
the raging sea as a Satanic manifestation, evidence of the
coexistence of Christ and Satan. Part VII is a hymn of praise
and benediction to the sea for the understanding and conse-
quent peace that it has made possible.

The language of the poem, especially the wordplay, and
some of the allusions require further comment.

In Part I "flaw" is used in the primary sense of squall or
sudden gust of wind, but since the "Clerk of the Weather" is
portrayed as a kind of clerk of court who lays down "the
weather-law," this word may be thought of as a legal term
signifying a defect in a legal paper that may nullify it. In
this way Melville slyly suggests the dubious validity of the
opinions of the "Clerk of the Weather" and underscores the
natural intelligence of the sea creatures. Cf. John 3:8.

"Orm from the schools" of Part II may be Orm, author of
Ormulum, a book of metrical homilies dating from A.D.
1200, of little other than philological interest. Melville's
sketch, "Daniel Orme," is about an old sailor, "a salt phi-
losopher, not lacking in a grim common sense."

Melville in Part III relates the ocean waves to the Blue
Ridge Mountains in order to contrast the acoustical qualities
of the mountains, which promote reverberations, with the
"liquid hills" that have no echo. A similar passage—in
"The Old Shipmaster and His Crazy Barn," one of the manu-
script poems not reprinted here—reads: "From the long hills
and hollows that make up the sea, / Hills and hollows where
Echo is none." See also *Clarel,* IV, xxxiv, 49. The silence of
the sea has been much remarked (cf. the "blank ocean," in
the fifth line of "In the Desert"). The "strain" to which the
sea does not respond is man's song and those things such as
his hopes and dreams for which he exerts himself.

The word "crest" in the second line of Part VI is an example of Melville's intricate use of language. The "crest" of the Dragon may be a plume of feathers such as that which adorns a helmet. But the ridge of a wave is its "crest," a meaning re-enforced by "billow" and "comb" in the sense of the curling crest of a wave (cf. "Curled in the comb"); and "crest" denoting a mountain peak is suggested through the presence of "Andean" and the opposition of the "heaven-challenging crest" and "the Mount" of Christ. Finally, "crest" suggests high spirits or pride, in this instance the pride of the satanic Dragon. The "dove in her nest" is a vague but provocative allusion. It recalls the dove of Genesis 8:8–12 by means of which "Noah knew that the waters were abated from off the earth," the dove as emblem of the Holy Spirit, and the qualities of peace, purity, and gentleness traditionally associated with the dove.

Part VII begins with an allusion to a passage from Revelation 7:1–3 in which "four angels standing on the four corners of the earth, holding the four winds of the earth, that the wind should not blow on the earth, nor on the sea, nor on any tree" and another angel calls to them "Saying, Hurt not the earth, neither the sea, nor the trees. . . ." The "pitiless breath" of the angels has been prefigured in the stormy winds of Part I, now tempered and made fragrant by the healing herb, rosemary. The botanical name for rosemary is *Rosmarinus*, literally sea-dew; hence Melville's reference to "wholesome dew," a distillate that restores physical and spiritual health. In ancient times rosemary was highly regarded for medicinal purposes. Its modern value is as a perfume, the oil being obtained by distillation.

BILLY IN THE DARBIES: from BILLY BUDD
[page 123]

At the close of 1885 when he retired after nineteen years as a customs inspector, Melville, according to a letter from his wife to a cousin, had "unfinished work at his desk" with which to occupy himself. Perhaps this work included an early draft of a short poem which he later called "Billy in the Darbies" and used as the conclusion to the novel, *Billy Budd*, uncompleted at the time of his death in 1891 and posthumously published. The careful study of the manuscript by Harrison Hayford and Merton M. Sealts, Jr., shows that the novel grew out of Melville's revisions and expansions of a headnote to this poem. Therefore in its origins it is related to "John Marr," which has a prologue considerably longer than the poem which it introduces, and to "Jack Roy" and "Tom Deadlight" in the same collection, both with brief headnotes giving the setting and biographical information. In fact one suspects that "Billy in the Darbies" would have found a place in *John Marr and Other Sailors* had not Melville amplified its headnote so extensively. By 1888, when *John Marr* was published, the poem and note had become a manuscript of some 150 pages and was still in a fairly early stage of development. What had happened was typical of Melville's method of composition—the working outward from a single idea, personal experience, object he had seen, or passage in a book he had read, until he had explored it to his satisfaction.

"Billy in the Darbies" is close to "Jack Roy" and "Tom Deadlight" in other ways. All three poems deal with simple sailors who are confronting death. Jack Roy, like Billy, is a kind of demi-god, capable of ascending from his resting place "fathoms down," a phrase repeated near the end of "Billy in the Darbies." Tom Deadlight, like Billy, sends greetings to the chaplain, asks for his tot of rum, and shakes the hand of a shipmate "before I roll over," here again language close to that in the final lines of "Billy in the Darbies." The three poems share a reminiscent quality and have in common a serene gravity lightened by touches of wry wit, including puns on the personal names of the title characters.

In a larger context, "Billy in the Darbies" is within the tradition of the broadside ballad. As the novel states, a "tarry hand made some lines which, after circulating among the shipboard crews for a while, finally got rudely printed at Portsmouth . . ." (Chapter 30). In *Redburn* (Chapter 39) Melville describes a disabled sailor who hawks broadside ballads along the Liverpool docks. The common subjects of such ballads included descriptions of the execution of felons, often emphasizing their admonitions, confessions, and bearing.

Among the possible literary sources are two quite different elegies well known to Melville: Milton's "Lycidas," on the drowning of a Cambridge classmate, and Charles Dibdin's "Tom Bowling," on the death of his sailor brother. The relevant passage in "Lycidas" occurs in the concluding consolation where the poet calls for a cessation of grief "For *Lycidas* your sorrow is not dead, / Sunk though he be beneath the watry floar." In the end Lycidas, his "oozy Locks" (cf. Melville's "oozy weeds") laved in nectar, is transformed into a sea deity. Tom Bowling's ascension is thus described:

> His form was of the manliest beauty,
> His heart was kind and soft;
> Faithful, below, he did his duty;
> But now he's gone aloft.

One of the more interesting parallels which these two poems share with "Billy in the Darbies" is the opposition of heights and depths, of "*Lycidas* sunk low, but mounted high" and Tom Bowling, once "under hatches" but now, according to the refrain, "gone aloft." In "Billy in the Darbies" this movement up and down, present in the language and action of the poem, suggests death and resurrection, a consolation, however, qualified by the harsh fact that Billy is raised on high by the hangman's rope and the possibility that the "oozy weeds" which twist about him as he sinks to sleep are fetters additional to the darbies which bind his wrists.

The nature of the vocabulary—a combination of the vernacular, romantic diction, and nautical terminology, often wittily manipulated—contributes richness and at the same time a sense of restraint. For example, Billy, musing on his imminent execution, thinks of himself as a "jewel-block"—a pulley suspended at the end of the main and fore topsail yards—which romantically shifts to a "Pendant pearl" like the rather realistic "ear-drop" he had given to Bristol Molly. These words have further associations. Billy is referred to by his former captain as a "jewel"; the root meaning of "pendant" is hanging; and "drop" is a synonym for the gallows. The references to the chaplain "down on his marrow-bones" and "nibble–bit o' biscuit" (though not "the last parting cup") have a colloquial cast that tends to obscure their function as suggestive of the last sacrament with its implications of immortality. In words which also have religious undertones, Billy had told the court, "I have eaten the King's bread and I am true to the King."

Cf. the final lines and Jonah's prayer (2:5): "The waters compassed me about . . . the depth closed me round about, the weeds were wrapped about my head." Jonah (1:12), like Billy, was a sacrificial victim cast into the sea.

Travel Long Ago

TIMOLEON [page 126]

Written late in his life, "Timoleon" is even more than most of Melville's poems a personal expression. It contains memories of his youth when, within the family circle, he was a poor second to his accomplished brother, Gansevoort; it raises metaphysical problems such as he had long brooded upon, to the perturbation of those closest to him; it reflects his responses—withdrawal and disdain for plaudits come late —to the lack of understanding he met with as a writer; and finally, it is yet another statement of opposition inherent in the human situation—conflicts between brother and brother, mother and son, ties of family and loyalty to the State, the laws of society and the higher law, the need for community and the integrity of the individual. The solution, rejection of Jove and Corinth for a life of repose as "the Isle's loved guest" (Part VIII), is really no solution at all but a posture assumed when it is recognized that there are oppositions which seem incapable of resolution and queries for which there seem to be no answers. Timoleon, however, has penetrated as deeply into the "core" (cf. "The Coming Storm") of his own nature as is humanly possible (Part VI), and he has fearlessly raised the ultimate questions (Part VII).

For the life of Timoleon (c. 411–c. 337 B.C.), the Corinthian statesman and general, Melville relied upon Plutarch's *Lives*, which he had read assiduously, and Pierre Bayle's *Historical and Critical Dictionary*, which he had bought in 1849. His departures from these two sources are mainly those of emphasis: a tendency to point up the family conflicts and to use the story as a vehicle to question the "Arch Principals" (Part VII) and man's position in relation to them.

Another source was the Balzac novel, *The Two Brothers* (Les Deux Poètes), published in 1887 in a new translation by Katherine Prescott Wormley. Among the pertinent passages which Melville marked are the following:

> Philippe, the elder of the two sons, was strikingly like his mother. Though a blond lad, with blue eyes, he had the daring look which is readily taken for intrepidity and courage. . . .

> Agathe believed that the purely physical resemblance which Philippe bore to her carried with it a moral likeness; and she confidently expected him to show at a future day her own delicacy of feeling, heightened by the vigor of manhood. . . .

> . . . Philippe, a captain at nineteen and decorated . . . flattered his mother's vanity immensely. Coarse, blustering, and without real merit beyond the vulgar bravery of a cavalry officer, he was to her mind a man of genius; whereas Joseph, puny and sickly, with unkempt hair and absent mind, seeking peace, loving quiet, and dreaming of an artist's glory, would only bring her, she thought, worries and anxieties.

The "Rammon" fragment (see note on "The Enviable Isles") also has a confrontation of brothers. The mild, philosophical Rammon pleads with his rash half-brother, Rehoboam, to restore order to the kingdom through generous peace terms and attention to the advice of experienced councilors. When Rehoboam disdainfully rejects his suggestions, Rammon "withdrew to his meditations."

AFTER THE PLEASURE PARTY   [page 132]

The difficulties which this powerful and complex lyric presents arise from its rich texture, its sometimes elliptical style, its private symbolism, its pattern of oppositions, its occasional ambiguities, and its shifts in place, time, and point of view. Structurally the poem consists of the introductory warning of Amor, god of love, followed by seventeen stanzas which may be divided into four sections. The first section (the

first twelve stanzas) has as its setting a terraced garden on
"the starlit Mediterranean." Here, until the stars "wane" and
"Light breaks," a woman who has devoted herself to intel-
lectual pursuits, particularly to "starry lore," recalls an experi-
ence which has forced her to probe her own nature and the
implications of her past life. While attending a "pleasure-
party" or rural excursion, she had felt a deep attraction to-
ward a man who had ignored her for a peasant girl. She is
shocked by the discovery of the strength of her sexuality and
wracked with jealousy and self-pity, but throughout her ex-
amination of the experience, she is ruthlessly honest with
herself. The second section (stanzas thirteen and fourteen)
has the poet as spokesman. He addresses the woman as
Urania, the muse of astronomy, warns her of the power of
Amor, and wonders whether she has been able to "forget"
the "pleasure-party." He then relates how he saw her at the
Villa Albani in Rome, gazing enraptured at a classical statue.
The third section (the fifteenth stanza) returns to the woman
who, in a different place tells how "To-day" a picture of the
Virgin Mary moved her to consider entering a nunnery. She
turns instead to the "armed Virgin," to whom she prays for
strength. The fourth section (stanzas sixteen and seventeen)
concludes the poem with a statement from the poet that
"Art" cannot sustain Urania for any long period and that
Amor will have "his vengeance." As a kind of counterpoint to
Urania's prayer to the "armed Virgin," he asks "virgins every-
where" to pray for her and be warned by her example.

The poem is essentially an expression of human limita-
tion stated in oppositions such as the astronomical imagery,
which represents dedication to intellectual accomplishment,
and the rose imagery, which is associated with sexual love;
the matters of "turbulent heart and rebel brain"; the "Chris-
tian heart" and "heathen Art"; the Virgin Mary and the
"armed Virgin," Athene. The insistence upon incompleteness
which the metaphor of virginity implies is most intense in the
eleventh stanza where Urania cries out that her sex makes her
a half-being, split apart from an original oneness by some
"Cosmic jest or Anarch blunder." Her outcry is not for herself
alone; she sees that "Few matching halves meet and mate."
This last quotation recalls Melville's "Art," a poem which

also has a sexual substratum, is presented in terms of opposi-
tions, and insists that a price must be paid for creativity.

In the end Urania, though shaken by her experience, re-
fuses "to kneel and believe," to accept the easy way for the
virgin bypassed by love. Instead she prays to a heathen god-
dess for strength to fight her battles.

By having the poet intrude in the final lines with a warn-
ing that Urania remains in a state of peril, Melville has the
best of both situations: sympathy for the tough valor of
Urania and agreement with the poet's warning against its
limitations.

There is fine irony as well as erotic connotation in the title.

THE NIGHT-MARCH   [page 137]

The radiant power of the army as it marches silently
through the night "in order true" is reminiscent of the "geo-
metric beauty" of the fleet in "Dupont's Round Fight." Mel-
ville was much concerned with the ultimate force which
made such order possible, but he found it difficult to commit
himself regarding its nature or even, as here, where he quali-
fies with the parenthetical phrase "So legends tell," of the
certainty of its existence. The contrast of the light that
emanates from the army with the darkness through which it
marches is effective symbolically and as a visual image.

THE RAVAGED VILLA   [page 137]

On February 20, 1857, Melville went from Naples to
Posillipo, recording in his travel journal that he had seen
"ruins of villas." A month later he visited Tivoli, eighteen
miles from Rome, and his journal for March 20, 1857, notes
his impressions: "Villa of Hadrian—Solemn scene & solemn
guide—Extent of ruin—fine site. Guide philosophising. . . .
Villa of Mecanas [sic]." The extensive ruins near Naples
date from the period of Augustus when the region was a
popular resort. A part of the ruins of the Villa of Maecenas,

when Melville saw them, was being used to house an iron-works.

Melville's recollections of "ruins of villas" found their way into "The Ravaged Villa," a title that emphasizes despoilment rather than the mere dilapidations of time. Classic beauty and wisdom, symbolized by "the laurel" of the poet and "Apollo's bust" seem to have come to a particularly ignoble end.

Melville owned an engraving by Robert Brandard of the ruins of the Villa of Maecenas after a painting by Richard Wilson that he may have seen when he visited the National Gallery in London.

THE MARGRAVE'S BIRTHNIGHT [page 138]

In this bitter Christmas ballad Melville portrays a world in which meaning has departed from ritual and from which the gods have withdrawn. Though not necessarily through any fault of their own, so debased are the peasants who have gathered to celebrate the birth of their "good lord" that they are satisfied by the bread and wine they receive for its own sake and cannot comprehend the miracle that it implies. The "Empty throne and vacant cover" clearly "Speak the absent lord" but his subjects are incapable of hearing him. They are animals, their sheepskin clothing consistent with their sheeplike behavior (though they are hardly lambs of God) and their comparison to plow horses with the brutal "toil and travail" of their daily existence. Their spiritual limitation is best seen through the account of Christ changing the water into wine (John 2:11) to which the last stanza refers: "This beginning of miracles did Jesus in Cana of Galilee, and manifested forth his glory; and his disciples believed on him." Note also the pun on "host."

THE GARDEN OF METRODORUS [page 140]

Metrodorus was the name of at least ten Greek philosophers or literary figures, five of whom Melville would have known from Pierre Bayle's *Historical and Critical Dictionary*. Among them Metrodorus of Chios, disciple of Democritus, who received the greatest attention from Bayle, and the Metrodorus described by Bayle as "Epicurus' friend," probably Metrodorus of Lampascus, would have interested Melville most. Metrodorus of Chios is best remembered for his radical skepticism, evident in such statements as "We know nothing, no, not even whether we know or not," the opening sentence of his *On Nature*. Bayle states that he "is reckoned among those who denied all certainty." Metrodorus of Lampascus, disciple and close friend of Epicurus, exceeded his master in dogmatically embracing the doctrine of pleasure. Melville owned an engraving by George Cooke from the *Historic Gallery of Portraits and Paintings*, Vol. IV (London, 1807–11) showing four heads. In the margin he wrote the names "Epicurus" and "Metrodorus."

The poem is a statement of the difficulty in obtaining a categorical answer to any question, and its form, appropriately, is a sequence of interrogatives. The silence and the overgrown paths of the garden are further indications of the limitations of knowing.

Melville suggests that the withdrawal into the silent, unkempt garden is in itself a puzzling response and raises more questions than it answers: for example, questions of whether the state of quietude is one of happiness or sadness, peace or sin. But he himself was sympathetic to withdrawal as the conclusion to the poem "Timoleon" attests. In his copy of Camoën's poetry he marked this passage from "Sonnet VI":

> My senses lost, misjudging men declare
> And Reason banish'd from her mental throne,
> Because I shun the crowd, and dwell alone.

IN A GARRET   [page 140]

Melville's journal of his travels in the Near East has repeated references to St. Sophia in Constantinople, one of the glories of Byzantine art. An entry dated December 13, 1856, reads: "Supurb [*sic*] interior. Precious marbles Porphyry &

Verd antique. Immense magnitude of the building." On December 17 he wrote: "Owing to its peculair [sic] form St: Sophia viewed near to, looks as partly underground; as if you saw but the superstructure of some immense temple, yet to be disinterred. You step *down* to enter."

The impression of the sumptuousness of the building is retained in the poem and the need to descend in order to enter it may lie behind the nautical imagery of grappling for objects from the depths of the sea. However, the word "grapple" also indicates the strain and conflict involved in plumbing the depths. Melville rejects great riches accumulated through the efforts of others for the opportunity to grapple for a single gem himself. If he had in mind the significance of the name St. Sophia, in English "Holy Wisdom," then the poem hints at an opposition between philosophy and art in the process of artistic creativity.

Titles which Melville considered but discarded include "Ambition," "Schiller's Ambition," and "The Spirit of Schiller." His copy of Schiller's *Poems and Ballads* in the translation of Edward Bulwer Lytton shows marked passages in "The Diver." This ballad is about a brave, ambitious squire who plunges into a maelstrom to recover a golden cup in response to the challenge of the king. When he succeeds, the king offers him the hand of his daughter if he dives for the goblet a second time. The squire does so and is drowned though he himself had warned that one should not "stretch too far the wide mercy of Heaven." "In a Garret" shares the idea of the risks involved in plunging for "One dripping trophy."

Echoes from "The Diver" also occur in "The Maldive Shark" and in the episode of the fall from the mainmast into the sea in *White-Jacket* (Chapter 92).

MONODY [page 141]

In August 1850 Melville reviewed *Mosses from an Old Manse* for *The Literary World*, revealing his profound grasp of Hawthorne's artistry and his sympathy for Hawthorne's ideas. Shortly thereafter the two men met. At about the same time they both moved to the Berkshire region of Massachusetts, Melville to Pittsfield and Hawthorne to nearby Lenox. The importance that Melville attached to their friendship is evidenced in his dedication of *Moby-Dick* "In token of my admiration for his genius . . . to Nathaniel Hawthorne," and, more poignantly, in a series of letters addressed to him in 1851 and 1852.

The first stanza of "Monody" was written soon after Hawthorne's death on May 19, 1864, and a date which was transcribed onto the title page of Melville's copy of Hawthorne's *Our Old Home* (1863). The allusion to "the cloistral vine" connects this poem to *Clarel* in which Vine, one of the principal characters, is in part a recollection of Hawthorne. While the poem was evoked by the memory of his friendship with Hawthorne and their subsequent estrangement, it becomes by extension a lament for the nature of human relationships, doomed as they are to limitations and misunderstandings.

LONE FOUNTS [page 141]

An examination of the manuscript shows that Melville considered two other titles—"Giordano Bruno" and "Counsels." The first seems especially pertinent to the sentiments of the poem for Bruno, a rebellious Italian Renaissance monk turned philosopher, suffered disillusion in his youth, was influenced by the older Greek philosophers, and was an original thinker who influenced Spinoza and others. He was excommunicated and burned at the stake by the Inquisition. His principal philosophical concern was the search for unity.

In this poem Melville again shows his interest in the limitations of youthful vision and the process that brings about enlightenment. Like "The Coming Storm," to cite a single example, it deals with the attainment of knowledge transcending the temporal and worldly to reach a state of timelessness that "forecloses" the possibility of "surprise," an expression common to both poems.

THE BENCH OF BOORS [page 142]

Melville's manuscript reveals that he dropped the words "Insomnia or" from the title and considered but rejected "Suggested by a Flemish picture" as a subtitle. He also considered and cancelled a note stating that "A particular picture is here referred to." An admirer of Dutch genre painting, he mentioned in his travel journal in 1857 "tavern scenes" and "Dutch convivial scenes" by David Teniers the Younger (1610–90) observed in museums at Turin and Amsterdam. Teniers was famous for his paintings of boors, Dutch peasants, in tavern settings. In "At the Hostelry," one of the poems in the posthumously published "Burgundy Club" group, Melville has a number of artists discussing the "picturesque" in painting. Adriaen Brouwer speaks to his compatriot:

> Hey, Teniers? Give us boors at inns,
> Mud floors—dark settles—jugs—old bins,
> Under rafters foul with fume that blinks
> From logs too soggy much to blaze
> Which yet diffuse an umberish haze
> That beautifies the grime, methinks.

The boors represent a lower but more tranquil level of existence than the higher intelligence but restlessness of the poet. The contrast is developed through two images, drowsiness and insomnia, supported by related images. Associated with drowsiness are mental dullness, warmth, physical well-being, compression of space, and dim light; associated with insomnia are mental acuity, chill, physical discomfort, spaciousness, and excessive light. In one of the "Fragments of a Lost Gnostic Poem of the 12th Century," Melville similarly opposed "indolence" and "energy."

THE ENTHUSIAST [page 143]

Despite its seeming kinship to Henley's poem, it is diffi-
cult to accept "The Enthusiast" as an endorsement of idealis-
tic affirmation, a kind of Melvillian "Invictus," for Melville
often presents a viewpoint other than his own, and he de-
fines and qualifies his attitude toward "enthusiasm" else-
where in his writings. Thus "A Utilitarian View of the Moni-
tor's Fight" depicts the battle of the ironclads as it appears
to a utilitarian, which Melville certainly was not, and another
Civil War poem, not included in this collection, "Stonewall
Jackson (ascribed to a Virginian)," is a tribute to the dead
Confederate general from a fellow Confederate and Virginian.

The word "enthusiast" in the original Greek means a per-
son inspired and possessed by the gods. In *Pierre*, a novel
about a young man who is destroyed by his idealism, Melville
identifies "the Enthusiast to Duty" with "the heaven-begotten
Christ" (Book V, Chapter 5) and describes the protagonist
as "our young Enthusiast" (Book IV, Chapter 1). Melville
was deeply moved by "enthusiasts" because he frequently
sympathized with their views and because he feared that the
tough realities of earthly existence would inevitably lead to
their destruction.

The epigraph is from Job 13:15, among the books of the
Bible a particular favorite of Melville's. It is the doctrine of
Father Mapple's great sermon in *Moby-Dick* (Chapter 9).

ART [page 144]

In no other poem does Melville state so explicitly his idea
of the nature of artistic creation. Only from opposites in
conflict, and only after struggle and sacrifice, is it possible to
produce the work of art. The artist's placid dreams cannot
give form or life to his ideas. To embody them he must bring
together opposing elements, active and passive, male and
female. Such words as "pulsed life" and "mate" give a bio-
logical tone to the process of artistic creation.

The poem moves from a state of passivity to intense activity, the pace increasing as the number of opposing elements in the lines increase. When these opposing elements are reconciled, they must become part of the patriarch Jacob whose victory over the angel gained him a blessing and a new name but also an injury in the hollow of the thigh (Genesis 32:24–32). Because this wound is symbolically an emasculation, the ironical aspects and exactions of creativity are made evident. The importance given the "unlike things" that must be brought together stresses Melville's idea of the fundamental complexity and variety inherent in all objects and concepts.

Cf. Coleridge on fusion and the "reconciliation of opposite or discordant qualities," *Biographia Literaria* (Chapter XIV).

BUDDHA [page 144]

As a note in the margin of a manuscript draft of this poem indicates, James 4:14 is the source of the epigraph. The same biblical passage appears in *White-Jacket* (Chapter 31), where it refers to the smoke from a frigate's guns fired as a tribute to a deceased secretary of the navy.

Though Melville's knowledge of Buddhism was superficial, his interest in Buddhist thought also appears in "Rammon," unfinished and not published at the time of his death. In this fragment, Rammon, "not mentioned in the canonic Scripture, the unrobust child of Solomon's old age," shows a familiarity with Buddhist ideas about death which are said to have reached the court of Solomon through the Queen of Sheba and commercial dealings with Hiram, King of Tyre.

The "dumb endurers" are significant because they recall the boors of "The Bench of Boors," the peasants of "The Margrave's Birthnight," and the slave woman of "Formerly a Slave," all of whom "endure" at a low level of existence and accomplishment.

FRAGMENTS OF A LOST GNOSTIC POEM
OF THE 12TH CENTURY   [page 145]

Gnosticism, a mystic religion that arose concurrently with Christianity, was characterized by an Oriental dualism. By the fourth century it had declined, as had the bulk of the writings of the Church Fathers against it, and had been largely superseded by the Manichean movement. Among the more important Gnostic fragments that have survived is the "Song of the Soul," incorporated in the apocryphal Acts of Thomas. It is attributed to Bardaisan, a third-century teacher of Christianity in Asia Minor who had close affinities to Gnosticism. Of Gnostic or other origin, such ideas as the positive power of evil and the limitation equally of active energy and passivity appealed to Melville.

THE MARCHIONESS OF BRINVILLIERS
[page 145]

As is not infrequently the case, Melville assumes the reader's knowledge of a somewhat obscure personage, and without such knowledge the poem appears to be little more than a graceful compliment to a lovely though somewhat mysterious lady. Marie Madeleine Marguerite d'Aubray, Marquise de Brinvilliers, was an infamous poisoner executed in 1676. The language of the poem and its point of view suggest that Melville had in mind a portrait of her. He may have remembered a crayon sketch by Charles Le Brun showing the marquise on her way to the scaffold. It was prominently displayed in the Louvre—which Melville visited on November 30, 1849—much remarked upon, and widely reproduced.

The Melville family library contained a copy of *The Letters of Madame de Sévigné* who left a memorable account of the execution in a letter to her daughter dated July 17, 1676:

All is over and Brinvilliers has ascended into the air: after the execution her body was cast into the flames of a great fire, and her ashes scattered to the winds. She is now part of the atmosphere we breathe, and when by means of little spirits we are overcome by poisonous fumes, we shall be greatly astonished. Judgment was finally passed yesterday, and the sentence was read to her this morning, which was that she should confess publicly at Notre-Dame, that she should have her head cut off, her body burned, and her ashes scattered to the winds. She was questioned under duress; but she said this was unnecessary, that she would confess all; and she did, taking nearly five hours of the evening to recount the story of her life, which was even more frightful than one had thought. She attempted to poison her father ten times (but was unable to bring it off), her brothers and several others; always mixed in with protestations of love and mutual confidences.

The various accounts of her life agree that the Marquise de Brinvilliers was an attractive little woman with a curious, childlike innocence about her. Melville was interested in both the outer appearance that was appropriate to the inner person—see, for example, "At the Cannon's Mouth" where the manly virtue of the naval hero, Lieutenant Cushing, is seen in his physical being, or Billy Budd and Claggart in *Billy Budd*—and the external appearance that was in direct contrast to internal reality, as in this poem.

In this poem Melville concentrates the enigma of the Marquise de Brinvilliers' appearance and behavior in the phrase, "Her fathomless mild eyes." The eyes of the mysterious, sensual Hautia of Melville's allegorical novel *Mardi*, are also "fathomless," but the heroic youth, Cushing, has "unfathomable eyes."

THE AGE OF THE ANTONINES [page 146]

An earlier version of "The Age of the Antonines" was enclosed in a letter dated March 31, 1877, from Melville to his brother-in-law, John Chapman Hoadley, who had sent him examples of his own poetry the week before. Melville wrote: "In return for you M.S. [*sic*] favors I send you something I found the other day—came across it—in a lot of papers. I remember that the lines were suggested by a passage in Gibbon (Decline & Fall) Have you a copy? Turn to 'Antonine' &c in index."

Antoninus Pius, adopted son of the Emperor Hadrian, reigned from A.D. 138 to 161. He was succeeded by Marcus Aurelius, his adopted son, who ruled until 180. The period was one of sound government and internal tranquillity. The first chapter of Edward Gibbon's *Decline and Fall of the Roman Empire*, and especially the important opening paragraph, seems pertinent:

> In the second century of the Christian era, the empire of Rome comprehended the fairest part of the earth, and the most civilized portion of mankind. The frontiers of that extensive monarchy were guarded by ancient renown and disciplined valour. The gentle, but powerful influence of laws and manners had gradually cemented the union of the provinces. Their peaceful inhabitants enjoyed and abused the advantages of wealth and luxury. The image of a free constitution was preserved with decent reverence: the Roman senate appeared to possess the sovereign authority, and devolved on the emperors all the executive powers of government. During a happy period of more than fourscore years, the public administration was conducted by the virtues and abilities of Nerva, Trajan, Hadrian, and the two Antonines.

The poem repeats several Melvillian themes: the decline of religious faith and political order; dim, distant hopes for the future; and a golden age in the classical past. It is more interesting, however, for revealing an attitude and approach which appeared increasingly in Melville's mature years. Instead of the intensity, magnitude, and irony so often evident in his writing, he sometimes favored smaller forms, a less pretentious touch, and a somewhat simple directness. Such poems (a number of the "Weeds and Wildings" come to mind) suggest that Melville, like the Antonines, had "reasoned of fate at the flowing feast," that is, had become realistic about the bounds of human knowledge and endeavor but was not blighted thereby. The letter to Hoadley concludes:

> You are young (as I said before) but I aint; and at my years, and with my disposition, or rather, constitution, one gets to care less and less for everything except downright good feeling. Life is so short, and so ridiculous and irrational (from a certain point of view) that one knows not what to make of it, unless—well, finish the sentence yourself.

In his lecture, "Statues in Rome," given on several occasions in 1857–59, Melville had observed that it was not unusual for Roman gentlemen at their feasts "to talk upon the subject of death and other mournful themes."

Melville owned engravings of Hadrian and Antoninus Pius by George Cooke from the *Historic Gallery of Portraits and Paintings*, Vol. III (London, 1807–11). Cf. *Clarel* (IV, xx, 48–60) on the Antonines.

HERBA SANTA [page 147]

Melville found comfort in tobacco and refers to smoking frequently in his letters. In the novels pipe smoking often has symbolic significance. In *Moby-Dick*, for example, Ishmael and Queequeg seal their pact of brotherhood by smoking the tomahawk pipe, which Ishmael first thought of as a dangerous weapon (Chapter 10), and Ahab throws his "lighted pipe into the sea" when he has changed so much that it can no longer bring him peace (Chapter 30).

References to the Indians' ceremonial use of tobacco ("Indian air," "tribal," "Calumet," "Pipe of Peace") contribute unity and meaning.

Because tobacco can bring peace and comfort, especially to the lowly, it is a holy herb. Its sacred nature is underscored in section V, the climax of the poem, where Melville associates the transcendent idea which tobacco represents with "Love supreme" or Christ, who, though rejected "as a god" and "As man," may yet "come . . . In likeness of a weed." The identification with Christ is prepared for in section II, where the communion supper ordained by "Love" leads to "strange new feuds," and is sustained throughout the poem by other religious references.

St. Martin's summer is late Indian summer. Cf. "Indian air." St. Martin's Day is November 11.

VENICE [page 149]

Melville visited Venice April 1–6, 1857, and his travel journal repeatedly mentions Venetian "palaces." In the poem he recognizes that a pantheistic energy is shared by the coral worm and mankind, resulting in "reefs of palaces" in the shallow lagoons of Venice and "marble garlandry" in the depths of the Coral Sea. Pan, the son of Hermes and chief of the satyrs, perhaps because his name means "all," came to be regarded in later times as a primitive force permeating all nature.

On March 23, 1857, Melville saw the Cathedral at Pisa, one end of which "looks like coral grottoes in sea. . . ."

IN A BYE-CANAL [page 150]

In his travel journal on April 5, 1857, Melville described a Venetian scene which may lie behind this poem: "Looked up and down G[rand] Canal. Wandered further on. Numbers of beautiful women. The rich brown complexions of Titian's women drawn from nature, after all. (Titian a Venetian) The clear, rich, golden brown. The clear cut features, like a cameo.—The vision from a window at end of long, narrow passage."

In the poem an empty, ominous silence recalling ocean calms before a storm or haunted nights like that when Jael, under the guise of hospitality, slew the beguiled Canaanite general, Sisera (Judges 4:2–23), characterizes the atmosphere of the canal. The faint noise of the boat arouses a response at the window of an ancient palace; eyes flash between the slats of the Venetian blind, eyes like those of the basilisk, that fascinate and are destructive. The passenger in the boat, because he has penetrated deeply into a variety of experiences—read the "portents in nature," swum between "the whale's black flukes and the white shark's fin," wandered in the wilderness, known the leprous company of "Envy and Slander," can step aside almost blithely from the "conjuration" of the "latticed eye." Possessed with a detachment attained through such experiences, he instructs the gondolier, who has been dreaming at his post, to speed from the scene of temptation. He then reflects on "the Naturalists" who, in their scientific simplemindedness, deny the existence of sirens, and with mild amusement at their reaction and at his own behavior when tempted by sirens, he remembers the example of the wily Ulysses under similar circumstances (*Odyssey*, Book XII).

The poem shifts drastically in form and tone (though not in theme), but Melville carefully provides devices that contribute to its unity. Note, for example, the progress from drugged indolence to alert wakefulness; the recurrent focus upon visual perception through words like "sight," "eyes," "glance," and "scanned"; the pattern of light and dark in the slats of the lattice as preparation for the contrast between the flukes of the whale and the fin of the shark; and the gradation of language from the heavy, portentous opening stanza to a second stanza of rather conventional narrative ending curiously with the discordant parallelism of the terminal couplet, to a third stanza that reaches a peak of intensity followed by an abrupt decline into the colloquial, to a concluding quatrain that seems spritely to an almost facetious degree until the final sonorous, stately line.

Ulysses, the favorite of Athene, goddess of wisdom, was not the "son" of Venus, goddess of beauty, but connotatively "Venus" suggests "Venice." He knew the hazards of venery.

The manuscript has this rejected subtitle: "(How it fared with a reputed libertine, as told me by himself.)" The last ten lines reveal echoes of Pope's translation of the *Odyssey* (Book XII), a copy of which Melville owned and annotated.

PISA'S LEANING TOWER   [page 151]

In Pisa on March 23, 1857, Melville saw the Cathedral, Baptistery, and Campanile or Leaning Tower. He wrote in

his travel journal: "Campanile like pine poised just ere snap-
ping. You wait to hear crash. Like Wordsworth's moon
cloud, it will move all together if it moves at all, for Pillars
all lean with it."

IN A CHURCH OF PADUA   [page 151]

Melville visited the Church of St. Anthony, the Giotto
chapel, and the nearby Church of the Eremintani when he
was in Padua on April 1, 1857. The confessional interested
him because it constituted an effort to understand and deal
with man's darker nature. Note the oppositions centering on
"without" and "within," and "here" and "there."

In "In the Turret," Lieutenant Worden, commander of the
Monitor, is said to be "Sealed as in a diving-bell," a device
that permits sounding the depths but also imprisons.

MILAN CATHEDRAL   [page 152]

The Duomo of Milan, a cathedral built of white Carrara
marble in the Gothic style, is the third largest church in
Europe. Its pointed roof is constructed of marble blocks and
is ornamented with rows of pinnacles, spires, and turrets sur-
mounted by statues. Melville visited the Milan Cathedral on
April 7, 1857, and made the following entry in his travel
journal: "Glorious. More satisfactory to me than St. Peters.
A wonderful grandure [sic]. Effect of burning window at
end of aisle. Ascended,—Far below people in the turrets of
open tracery look like flies caught in cobweb.—The groups
of angels on points of pinnacles & everywhere. Not the con-
ception but execution. View from sumit [sic]. Might well
[illegible word] host of heaven upon top of Milan Cathe-
dral."

The poem describes an impressive building, extravagantly
rich in its decoration, set in a lush and ancient land. The
arrangement of the statues of the saints prevents this abun-
dance from leading to heaviness or disorder. The effect is
artistically successful because the "synodic hierarchies" of

statuary reflect the sublime order of the heavenly host. In "Dupont's Round Fight," Melville expressed a similar view of the essential unity, based upon order, of art and religion.

THE PARTHENON [page 153]

Seen aloft from afar. An entry in the travel journal dated February 8, 1857, records Melville's impression of the Acropolis seen by moonlight as he drove from Piraeus to Athens. On the return journey three days later he noted the "Acropolis in sight nearly whole way. Straight road. Fully relieved against the sky."

Nearer viewed. Lais was the name of two Greek courtesans of exceptional beauty about whom there is some confusion and to whom are attached a number of anecdotes. The name was used as a generic term for a courtesan, which suggests a deliberately meretricious quality in Lais' beauty appropriate to this poem. The Parthenon, considered the finest example of Doric architecture, has "curved" cornices and "inclined" columns, in order to adjust for optical distortion. Thus, like Lais, its effect depends upon an artful "subtlety." That the Parthenon literally means chamber of the virgin (i.e., Athena) adds a piquant touch which Melville may or may not have intended. Spinoza, a philosopher passionately devoted to the search for unity, would have seen a shared substance in the quite different modes or forms of the Greek building and the courtesan. Melville contributes to the theme of unity by addressing the building as if it were a person. At one point in the draft, he considered substituting "The Pantheist" for "Spinoza."

The Frieze. Melville had in mind the sculpture from the Parthenon frieze, which shows horsemen and figures bearing amphorae. He mentions the horses in his lecture of 1857–59 on "Statues in Rome." He probably saw the Elgin Marbles, a collection that includes sections of this frieze, during his several visits to the British Museum in London in 1849 or had at hand one of the many prints of the frieze available at the time. Characteristically, he notes the tensions between the delicately prancing horses and their solemn riders as opposed to the maidens with the pitchers who are both meek or subdued and "bright." The poem "Art" also presents an aesthetic based upon the fusion of contraries.

The last Tile. Ictinus is reputed to have been the architect of the Parthenon, the most important building that Pericles commissioned for the Acropolis. Aspasia was Pericles' mistress. In *Pierre* (Book XIV, Chapter 1) Melville begins a significant passage on silence: "All profound things, and emotions of things are preceded and attended by Silence." In the journal of his visit to London dated November 24, 1849, he observed of silence that "the old Greeks deemed it the vestibule to the higher mysteries."

GREEK MASONRY [page 155]

Melville wrote in his travel journal on February 8, 1857, following the underscored word "*Acropolis*": "Imperceptible seams—frozen together." A similar reference occurs in the journal two days later: "Pavement of Parthenon—square—blocks of ice. (frozen together.)—No morter [*sic*]: Delicacy of frostwork." He considered but discarded two titles for the poem, "The Masonry in Greek Temples" and "The Chrystalline [*sic*] in Greek Temples." The latter title is interesting because it retains his association of marble with ice, present in the above quotations and elsewhere in the travel journal. In the same connection, a canceled third and fourth line read: "Painstaking in their art divine / Who wrought such temples chrystalline."

As in another statement of his aesthetic, "Dupont's Round Fight," Melville is asserting that formal order is the ultimate source of art, the "geometric beauty" of the naval maneuver in "Dupont's Round Fight" having a counterpart in the "symmetry" of this poem.

Melville end-stops the first line where a run-on line is expected. This forces emphasis on the word "Together," which augments the idea of unity in the poem. At the same time, however, because of the element of enjambment still present, an excessive degree of rhyme is prevented.

GREEK ARCHITECTURE [page 155]

In *Billy Budd* Melville represents Captain Vere as having said: " 'With mankind . . . forms, measured forms are everything; and that is the import couched in the story of Orpheus with his lyre spell-binding the wild denizens of the wood.' " But as this poem reveals, he considered "Site," applied specifically to the architectural setting and broadly to the consideration of appropriate time and place in any art form, and "the Archetype," the fundamental rather than the ingenious or idiosyncratic, equally important.

Melville's travel journal indicates that he found in Greek architecture sustaining concepts, somewhat offsetting the dearth of such sustenance in what he had seen when he visited the Holy Land.

OFF CAPE COLONNA [page 156]

Cape Colonna, ancient Sunium Promontorium, a landmark for ships approaching Athens and a notorious hazard to navigation, is a rocky promontory on the southern coast of Attica. On its crest are the columns and other remains of a Temple to Poseidon, the sea god, built in the time of Pericles. This dramatic site attracted many nineteenth-century poets, among them Byron whose complete works Melville owned. Byron mentions Cape Colonna and the temple in *The Giaour, Don Juan*, and *Childe Harold*, attaching this note to Canto III of the latter: "In all Attica, if we except Athens itself and Marathon, there is no scene more interesting than Cape Colonna. . . . for an Englishman, Colonna has yet an additional interest as the actual spot of Falconer's shipwreck."

As a young officer in the merchant service, William Falconer was one of three survivors when his ship was wrecked off Cape Colonna in a severe storm. This experience is the subject of his once popular poem, *The Shipwreck* (1762), from which Melville quotes in the "Extracts" which preface

Moby-Dick. In *White-Jacket* (Chapter 65) he refers to "Falconer, whose 'Shipwreck' will never founder. . . ."

The columns of the temple at Sunium are equated with the gods in the majesty of their appearance and in the "serene" detachment with which they regard the shipwrecks that occur on the rocks below. In "Pebbles" (V) Melville describes the sea as "serene . . . not appeased, by myriads wrecks. . . ."

Another reference to the Sunium temple occurs in *Clarel* (I, xxxi, 12).

THE APPARITION [page 156]

Concerning the Acropolis, Melville wrote in his travel journal on February 8, 1857: "Parthenon elevated like cross of Constantine." (For other impressions of the Parthenon, see notes on "The Parthenon" and "Greek Masonry.") Until it was supplanted by the Cross that converted Constantine and with him the classical world, the Parthenon (built c. 438 B.C.) was the most appropriate "Trophy" of mankind because it represented his noblest achievement. It existed as a testing and shaping force. Had the philosopher Diogenes lived beneath its sway, he might have been less cynical.

As in "The House-top," Melville is playing on the word "cynic," which means dog in Greek. The Cynic philosophers took the dog as their badge, and when Diogenes died in 323 B.C., the Corinthians are said to have erected in his honor a column surmounted by a dog of Parian marble. He was, in fact, alive when the Parthenon was built.

A discarded version of the second stanza, revealing reconsiderations of his response to having seen the Parthenon, reads:

> With kindred power, appealing down,
>   Miraculous human Fane!
> You strike with awe the cynic heart,
>   Convert it from disdain.

THE ARCHIPELAGO [page 157]

As he sailed the Aegean Sea, Melville made a series of entries in his journal that are reflected in this poem. On December 23, 1856, he wrote: "Many other isles scattered about. Among others, Delos, of a most barren aspect, however flowery in fable." On December 26, 1856, he wrote: "Contrast between the Greek isles & those of the Polynesian archipelago. The former have lost their virginity. The latter are fresh as at their first creation. The former look worn, and are meagre, like life after enthusiasm is gone. The aspect of all of them is sterile & dry. Even Delos whose flowers rose by miracle in the sea, is now a barren moor, & to look upon the bleak yellow of Patmos, who would ever think that a god had been there." On February 5, 1857, he wrote: "In among the Sporades all night. . . . Patmos is pretty high, & peculiarly barren looking. No inhabitants.—Was here again afflicted with the great curse of modern travel—skepticism. Could no more realize that St: John had ever had revelations here, than when off Juan Fernandez, could believe [*sic*] in Robinson Crusoe according to De Foe."

Melville associates Delos, sacred as the birthplace of Apollo, the sun god, with Patmos, where St. John the Evangelist wrote the Book of Revelation. Alexander Selkirk was the original of Robinson Crusoe, a figure Melville repeatedly refers to in his writings. Melville first saw Juan Fernández, about four hundred miles west of Valparaiso, Chile, in May 1841, while serving on the whaler *Acushnet* and again in November 1843, as an ordinary seaman aboard the frigate *United States*.

Theseus, the great Athenian hero, landed at Delos and celebrated his victory over the Cretan Minotaur. His comparison to Sir Walter Raleigh has mild justification in that both ventured into little known lands but can best be accounted for through the connotations of the words "Virginia" and "Unravished." For Melville's thoughts on the "virginity" of the Greek Islands, see above.

Melville's memories of the Marquesas and elsewhere in

Polynesia are preserved mainly in the early novels *Typee* and *Omoo*. The poem is not so much an expression of nostalgia for the golden age of Pan or Polynesia as it is recognition of the indelible impress of primal splendor that the Greek isles retain despite the ravages of time.

IN THE DESERT [page 158]

From Cairo Melville went into the desert to see the pyramids, an experience that affected him deeply and led to a lengthy, detailed account in his journal dated January 3, 1857, from which the following is taken: "A long billow of desert foreevr [forever] hovers as in act of breaking, upon the verdure of Egypt. . . . Desert more fearful to look at than ocean."

The poem is framed through contrasting the Egyptian Plague of Darkness of the first stanza (Exodus 10:21) with the dazzling light of the desert, a "Shekinah" or holy manifestation of God's presence. The flaming radiance, which reaches its height in the last stanza, increases gradually and at times subtly. For example, "flamen" means priest but inevitably suggests flame as does "oriflamme," a banner of red silk attached to a lance, which in the poem connects with "fiery standard."

The last stanza has Miltonic undertones, recalling the invocation, "Hail holy Light, . . . Bright effluence of bright essense increate" (*Paradise Lost*, Book III, ll. 1–6) and, less directly and inverted, the anguished outcry of blind Samson, "O dark, dark, dark, amid the blaze of noon." (*Samson Agonistes*, l. 80.)

Weeds, Wildings, and Roses

THE LITTLE GOOD FELLOWS   [page 160]

The robin comes in the spring as a bridegroom, offering love to man in return for love. He protests his usefulness to man, arguing that those who love robins thrive, that it is the practice of robins to cover the friendless dead to prevent the desecration of their bodies, and that robins chase away the winter. In exchange he asks permission to inhabit the orchards unmolested, to live in a state of natural affinity with man like that of "grass to stones." The poem, therefore, is a plea for the oneness of man with nature, for man to adapt himself to the harmony of nature manifest in the cycle of the seasons.

The source of the second stanza is the dirge from John Webster's *The White Devil* (V, iv, 95–104):

> Call for the Robin Red-brest and the wren,
> Since ore shadie groves they hover,
> And with leaves and flowres doe cover
> The friendlesse bodies of unburied men.
> Call unto his funerall Dole
> The Ante, the field-mouse, and the mole . . .

Melville also echoes Webster's dirge in the thirteenth stanza of "The Armies of the Wilderness."

CLOVER   [page 160]

While the clover fields are "Rosier" and the breast of the ruddock or robin is "Ruddier" because they take on added color from "Dawn's red flush," their coloration is also a buoyant salute to the break of a summer day.

One suspects that Melville had in mind as a counterpoint to the calculated unpretentiousness of this quatrain such apostrophes to Dawn as the opening passage of Book V of Milton's *Paradise Lost* which begins: "Now Morn her rosie steps in th'Eastern Clime . . ."

A loose leaf among Melville's manuscripts has the heading "Clover" and the following lines: "Ye field flowers! the garden's eclipse you, 'tis true, / Yet wildings of nature I doat upon you / Campbell." They are the beginning lines of Thomas Campbell's "Field Flowers."

TROPHIES OF PEACE   [page 161]

In the spring of 1840, following an unrewarding season as a schoolteacher in Greenbush, New York, Melville left for a visit with his Uncle Thomas Melville in Galena, Illinois. By November he had returned to New York City and the following month he shipped out on the whaler *Acushnet*. Much later, during his lecture tour of 1859 he filled engagements in Chicago, Rockford, and Quincy, Illinois. The poem reflects his memories of the western prairies with their rich harvest. It rises somewhat above a pious hope mainly as a result of such phrases as "Files on files," "hosts of spears," and "rustling streamers" which are made to apply to both "the field" of battle and of corn, to Mars the war god and Ceres, goddess of agriculture.

FIELD ASTERS   [page 161]

The aster, because of its shape, derives its name from the Greek word meaning star. Melville, in raising the problem of seeing, does so through a characteristic reversal: the inscrutable "eyes" of the asters return the scrutiny of the "stargazers" without yielding up the secret of "their cheer." The verses seem to imply that the "cheer" of simple wildflowers should be accepted without too much ado, and perhaps they should not be made to bear the weight of further examination. However, Melville used the words "mystery starred in open skies" in his poem about the lovely little poisoner, "The Marchioness of Brinvilliers," who, he said, had "fathomless mild eyes." In "Field Asters" his interest is in the cause of good (though he was usually more concerned with the cause of evil) rather than with deceptive surface appearances.

THE AMERICAN ALOE ON EXHIBITION
[page 162]

The aging Melville's musings on his loss of an audience appear just beneath the surface of this poem. Reference to the flowering of the aloe as a revelation requiring prolonged waiting appear in *Clarel* (III, xxvii, 137) and in a letter to Evert Duyckinck dated February 2, 1850. In *Mardi* "the aloe flower, whose slow blossoming mankind watches for a hundred years" is considered a prize fit for a king (Chapter 164).

The century plant in the poem is indifferent to the ignominy of being displayed for the benefit of a few seekers after the curiosity of the moment. Years of waiting have given it a perspective beyond "joy and pride." It blames no one for having bloomed so late but cannot help remembering, though in so remote a way as to be without malice, the dead roses that considered it a weed.

ROSARY BEADS   [page 163]

Melville was attracted by the variety of symbolism accumulated about the rose, and he himself used the rose in various symbolic ways. For example, in the allegorical novel *Mardi*, the rose functions as part of the "language of flowers" from the nineteenth-century floral dictionaries, and it is associated with the sensuality of the enchantress and her handmaidens and the effusions of the poet. In *Clarel* (III, xiv, 33–40) among other things the rose, as in "The Rosary," is a symbol of transitory beauty from which lasting beauty may arise. Melville made a similar point in an unfinished sketch, "Under the Rose." Its Persian setting establishes connections with the ideas represented by roses in the *Rubáiyát* of Omar Khayyám, known to Melville in FitzGerald's translation.

For "Weeds and Wildings" Melville selected a group of eleven poems on the rose theme, including "Amoroso," "The New Rosicrucians," "Rose Window," and "Rosary Beads," all of which play upon the connotations and significations of their titles. Thus "Rosary Beads," though close to the language and melancholy hedonism of the *Rubáiyát*, is invested by its title with a touch of sanctity.

The rose as a symbol of feminine sexuality occurs in "After the Pleasure Party" where the woman who suppresses her inclinations is said to "tell such beads" on the "Sad rosary of belittling pain."

In his later years Melville grew roses and presented bouquets and dried petals to his intimates.

A *Fate Subdued*

IMMOLATED   [page 166]

The Melville family moved to Pittsfield, Massachusetts, in February 1850, and returned to New York in October 1863. In the house cleaning preparatory to their departure, Melville burned a number of manuscripts. The poem suggests that they belonged to the period of his young manhood and to a rural setting that he cherished. The immolated manuscripts were children of "Hope," and in assigning them to the bonfire, Melville protests that he was saving them from neglect, misunderstanding, and scorn. As a public literary person, he was shortly to choose for himself a like "fate subdued."

THE RUSTY MAN   [page 167]

Melville bought *Don Quixote de la Mancha* in a translation by Charles Jarvis in 1855, and in "The Piazza," a sketch written to introduce *The Piazza Tales* (1856), he refers to Don Quixote as "that sagest sage that ever lived." A particular sympathy for the Knight of La Mancha is to be expected from Melville, who shared Cervantes' concern for the nature of reality, the decline of values, the inroads of complacent utilitarianism, and the dignity of man.

The manuscript shows revision, including the cancellation of the original ninth line, which read "Seek the San Graal's light." In the eighth line Melville substituted *"wronged one's"* for "beggar's" and in the eleventh "grocer green" for "Philistine."

CAMOËNS   [page 168]

Luis de Camoëns (1524–80), whose epic on the voyages of Vasco da Gama, the *Lusiads*, brought him fame, died in poverty of the plague in a Lisbon hospital. In *White-Jacket* (Chapter 64) Melville has Jack Chase express great admiration for the *Lusiads*, which he twice quotes. Apparently as a young man Melville had read the epic in William Julius Mickle's translation. He acquired Strangford's edition of Camoëns in 1867, and has a reference to the Portuguese poet in *Billy Budd* (Chapter 8), his last work.

Like "The Rusty Man" and "The Ravaged Villa," this is an anti-utilitarian poem. It bitterly decries the baseness of a world to which the poet, in response to what he sees as the demands of God, has given his best and, having in the process spent his energies, is prey to those less dedicated than himself.

In the manuscript the word "Tasso" is written beside the captions of both parts of this poem. Melville owned a print of Torquato Tasso (1544–95), the Italian epic poet whose *Jerusalem Delivered* has as its subject the First Crusade. Tasso's career, consisting of initial success followed by a pathetic decline, was particularly interesting to Melville. According to his travel journal, Melville visited "Tasso's home" at Sorrento on February 22, 1857, "Tasso's prison" at Ferrara on March 31, 1857, and "St. Onofrio, church & monastery, where Tasso expired" at Rome on March 9, 1857. In his copy of Madame de Staël's *Germany* he marked this passage: "The morbid sensibility of Tasso is well known, as well as the polished rudeness of his protector Alphonso, who, professing the highest admiration for his writings, shut him up in a mad-house, as if that genius which springs from the soul were to be treated like the production of a mechanical talent, by valuing the work while we despise the workman."

The much revised manuscript shows an opening couplet which Melville cancelled: "And ever must I fan this fire? / Forever in flame on flame aspire?" In the last line he cancelled both "epic" and a second choice, "ancient."

Cf. the *Odyssey* (Book XII) in Pope's translation where Circe advises Ulysses not to attack the sea monster, Scylla:

> O worn by toils, O broke in fight,
> Still are new toils and war thy dire delight?
> Will martial flames for ever fire the mind,
> And never, never be to Heaven resign'd?

A REASONABLE CONSTITUTION   [page 169]

The manuscript has this note by Melville: "Observable in Sir Thomas More's 'Utopia' are First[,] Its almost entire reasonableness. Second[,] Its almost entire impracticality[.] The remark applies more or less to the Utopia's prototype[,] 'Plato's Republic.'"

MONTAIGNE AND HIS KITTEN   [page 170]

In a letter dated October 5, 1885, to Ellen Marett Gifford, Melville wrote of a photograph of himself: "What the deuse [*sic*] makes him look so serious, I wonder. I thought he was of a gay and frolicsome nature, judging from the little rhyme of his about a Kitten. . . ." The poem belongs to his old age, when he professed to cherish simple pleasures and to enjoy foolishness. Montaigne suited his frame of mind, though allusions to the essayist occur in his works early and late, from *White-Jacket* to *Billy Budd* (Chapter 7). He bought a copy of Montaigne's *Essays* in 1848.

Melville envisions Montaigne, who was decorated with the Order of St. Michael in 1571, as putting such temporal rewards in their proper perspective.

In *Mardi* (Chapter 94) Melville speculates that there is no "creature, fish, flesh, or fowl, so little in love with life as not to cherish hopes of a future state."

A dizzard is a jester or court fool. Cf. *Clarel*, II, xxvii, 141.

The poem is in the tradition of Erasmus' *The Praise of Folly*.

HEARTS-OF-GOLD [page 171]

In the mid-1870s Melville wrote a series of prose sketches about a fictional "Burgundy Club," creating a framework and spokesmen for a projected book of light verse. As was his practice, he drew up tentative title pages and experimented with names for his imaginary organization, among them the "Falernian Odd Fellows Club" and the "Horatian Odd Fellows Club." These names occur in the poem.

The "Burgundy Club" sketches also mention the Persian lyric poet Hafiz, incidentally a notable winebibber and composer of drinking songs, and the genial, clubbable Horace. Melville had read the poetry of Pierre-Jean de Béranger as early as 1860, and in a letter to his cousin Abraham Lansing, in 1877, he says of a volume of Béranger: "a shabby little cask it is, but then, the contents!"

For Melville, wine, Burgundy or Falernian, represented geniality, a quality in short supply in the rather withdrawn life that he led at the time. It has been surmised that his desire for a more sociable situation contributed to the conception of the imaginary convivial club. For a mature expression of his attitude on good-fellowship, see the poem "The Age of the Antonines" and its Comment.

PONTOOSUCE [page 172]

Pontoosuc, a lake just north of Pittsfield, Massachusetts, held great attraction for Melville, and the poem is a recollection of the lake and the surrounding countryside. The landscape has similarities with the one Melville describes in "The Piazza" sketch. There, his account of the view from the piazza of his house at Pittsfield is also autumnal; it refers to the sweetness of the day; includes fields, pastures, orchards, uplands, lonely roads, and an excursion into "a fairy-land"; and mentions a flower "in starry bloom, but now, if you removed the leaves a little, showed millions of strange, cankerous worms" that seems to be connected with the lines here, "In very amaranths the worm doth lurk, / Even stars, Chaldaeans say, have left their place."

The opening lines of "Pontoosuce" recall the beginning of "Off Cape Colonna" with its vista of the columns of the Greek temple that "crown the foreland" and overlook the sea. The resemblance is superficial, however, because "Pontoosuce" is not an outcry against the gods who are aloof from the troubles of man but an expression of calm acceptance attained through the agency of a sympathetic goddess who explains that, while "All dies,"—whether tree, poem, noble deed, or truth—all is reborn. From the decay of the fallen pine on the forest floor rises the seedling. The "wedded" elements of "light and shade," of "warmth and chill," and of "life and death" form part of the primordial cycle of existence.

The manuscript shows that Melville considered calling this poem "The Lake."